Anyone wanting to make a lasting difference in this world will find value in *Conscious Wealth*. Brandon Hatton's insightful stories and lessons about wealth creation will help you get in touch with your mindset around money so that you can focus on what matters most!

—BOB CHAPMAN, chairman and CEO of Barry-Wehmiller, author of *Everybody Matters: The Extraordinary Power of Caring for Your People Like Family*

Brandon Hatton's book is a thought-provoking read that will change the way you think about money, improve your life, and make the world a better place. Brandon will teach you how to take control of your life and find real happiness by redefining your relationship with money, not the other way around.

—SAFWAN SHAH, CEO of PayActiv Inc.

In his book, *Conscious Wealth*, Brandan Hatton provides a contemporary answer to the ancient question: *Why do people who have so much, feel so little?* A highly engaging storyteller, Hatton weaves together an instructive narrative from his personal and professional life as well as solid empirical data. It's an important addition to the field of private wealth management and Conscious Capitalism.

—DR. PAUL HOKEMEYER, author of *Fragile Power*

Through personal stories and his practical experience as a wealth manager, Brandon Hatton bridges the gap between family coaching and wealth management. It's refreshing to see a humble, intentional, and mindful approach to wealth. If you are looking to move from merely having "enough" to having greater significance, *Conscious Wealth* is for you.

—ELLEN ROGIN, CPA, CFP, author of the *New York Times* bestseller *Picture Your Prosperity*

# CONSCIOUS
# WEALTH

# CONSCIOUS
# WEALTH

Money, Investing, and a Financial Awakening
for the Person Who Has It All

CONSCIOUS
CAPITALISM
PRESS™

BRANDON
HATTON

CAP, CRPC

**Conscious Capitalism Press**
www.consciouscapitalism.org/press

**Round Table Companies**
*Packaging, production, and distribution services*
www.roundtablecompanies.com

Deerfield, IL

| | |
|---|---|
| **Editing** | Mary Anna Rodabaugh, Holly Lorincz |
| **Cover Design** | Oust (www.weareoust.co), Christy Bui |
| **Interior Design** | Christy Bui, Sunny DiMartino |
| **Proofreading** | Carly Cohen |

Printed in the United States of America

First Edition: October 2021
10  9  8  7  6  5  4  3  2  1

**Library of Congress Cataloging-in-Publication Data**
Conscious wealth: money, investing, and a financial awakening for the person who has it all / Brandon Hatton.—1st ed. p. cm.
ISBN Paperback: 978-1-950466-30-6
ISBN Digital: 978-1-950466-31-3
Library of Congress Control Number: 2021940930

Conscious Capitalism Press is an imprint of Conscious Capitalism, Inc.
The Conscious Capitalism Press logo is a trademark of Conscious Capitalism, Inc.

Round Table Companies and the RTC logo are trademarks of
Writers of the Round Table, Inc.

## DISCLAIMER

All views expressed in this book are those of the author at the time of publication and do not represent the opinion of any other entity with which the author has been, is now, or may in the future be affiliated. The purpose of this book is to educate and inform, but it does not constitute financial advice or service.

The author makes no such warranties, express or implied, regarding the contents of this book. To the fullest extent permitted by applicable law, in no event will the author or his affiliates be liable for any damages, including without limitation, direct, indirect, incidental, special, consequential, or punitive damages, whether under contract or any other theory of liability, arising in connection of the use of the information in this book.

To my parents, Marlene and Duane Hatton.

. . . .

# CONTENTS

# INTRODUCTION

**"What is the purpose of finance?"**

The auditorium full of undergrads shuffle and roll their eyes at me. Some stifle groans.

I grip the podium, just as frustrated as they are. *These kids are majoring in finance! How can they think this is a stupid question?!* Whenever I have been asked to guest lecture, the response to this question is always the same.

"Come on . . . somebody, what is the purpose of finance?"

Finally, a hand will raise and I snap at the opportunity: "You!"

"To make money."

"Nope. You!"

"To build businesses."

"No again. Come on! You're finance majors! Does anybody know the point of your $70K annual tuition?"

No one ever does. It's very disappointing. So, I explain to them that most people believe the purpose of finance, or money, for that matter, is to make more money—and that is a myth. That belief system is exactly what got us into the 2008 financial crisis, the worst financial crisis in a century. The problem with the Financial Crisis of 2007–2008 was not that we had a recession; those happen more or less once a decade. No, the problem was that big banks, mortgage companies, insurance companies, Realtors, home buyers, industry individuals at all levels, and institutions committed fraud! They lied to *make more money* and believed (or didn't care) that their lies would not hurt anybody who mattered. They believed in the myth that we are all separate. They believed in externalities.

The purpose of finance is not to make money.

"Anybody else?" I will ask again, scanning the room for eager eyes. At this point, there are usually no takers, so I give them a hint. "The purpose of finance is the same purpose as everything else. It is the same as the purpose of, say, medicine."

Still no answers. Finally, I will sigh and give in.

"The purpose of finance is to make us better human beings. It is to allow companies time to develop new drugs for cancer or Alzheimer's; it is to build buildings that allow businesses to grow; it is to improve our lives in ways that eventually allow us to be healthy, happy human beings. Otherwise, why waste our time?"

At least they are sitting up by this point. Usually. A handful of go-getters will be taking notes.

"I went down to the med-school on campus to grab some Band-Aids earlier today. There was someone in there with what looked like a bad burn. Do you think he'd want to hear one of the doctors say that the purpose of medicine is to make money, or would he want a doctor who's more interested in caring for those who are suffering, or even saving lives?"

After a proper scolding, I always follow up with a second big question.

"What is the purpose of investing?"

Feeling chastised, the students usually go silent. Or the brave ones will venture what seems to be a common-sense guess: "To make the world better?"

Again, the answer is no. I let them take a few stabs at it, but nobody wants to say the obvious answer.

So, I give it to them.

"The purpose of investing is to make money! You don't invest to lose money. And the best way to make a buck is to invest in companies that want to make the world better. These companies understand that long-term value is created when they improve the lives of everyone.

*Enough proselytizing*, I think. *Time to get down to business.*

"I'm here today to provide you with a framework, and a mindset, around money and investments that will allow you to focus on what matters: a life of growth and fulfillment for yourself, your family, and the world around you." I pause to give them time to take notes. "We are going to talk about the four levels of what I call Conscious Wealth . . ."

. . . .

When I started out in the world of finance, right in the midst of the Great Recession rubble, I was untrusted and inexperienced. I was selling put options in order to pay for my monthly expenses, so I wasn't rolling in the dough—and yet my value proposition was *If you give me money, I will give you more.* This value proposition was, of course, absurd and absolutely not true. Unbeknownst to me as a naive rookie, it was also completely out of my ability to always make true, no matter how hard I tried.

Now? I am the senior vice president of investments at the Hatton Group. At least, that is my official title. I have also been called a financial advisor, financial planner, and wealth manager. I like to think of myself as an investment manager with the widest possible definition of investments. I manage portfolios of stocks, bonds, and private equity for clients, but I also provide advice on their businesses, children, philanthropy, estate plans, taxes, marriage, and divorce. You name it. I am like the Godfather's consigliere who doesn't actually kill anybody. I liked Robert Duvall's character in the movie, actually. He was the outsider, the adopted Irishman with a big heart. He always had a seat at the table.

Over the course of my career, I eventually figured out (sometimes the hard way) that my industry is full of nontruths, most of which tend to support the big players and leave the customers or "little guys" insecure. That is the secret sauce of the industry—fear. If the client is made to feel insecure, they will continue to pay for services. I too was afraid and insecure. I worked tirelessly for years with the threat of failure and poverty hanging over me. I defined success from that place of fear; yet, when I actually achieved financial security and was no longer afraid, the gains suddenly looked like fool's gold. I had no use for them. The path to that wealth creation had involved destruction. And it almost broke me, body and spirit.

Luckily, my clients are some of the most intelligent and accomplished individuals in this world, many of whom have decades more life experience than me. They have provided *me* guidance and wisdom, sometimes without even knowing it. Because of them, and my own burning desire to succeed while growing as a human, I made it to the other side.

As a successful investment manager, I now put the typical clients into two big groups. I have had clients who lived in fear, who did not have a strong sense of purpose, and who did not really think beyond themselves and their immediate family—I started to see them as rich. And I have had other clients with the same amount or less money than the rich clients, but lived with ease, a sense of purpose, and a desire to improve the world.

Coming to this realization was the beginning of what I call *Conscious Wealth*. This philosophy of living holistically has helped me, personally, go from being rich and fearful to being wealthy and fearless.

I've taught Conscious Wealth concepts to clients for years, as well as providing investment advice to nourish their migration toward this wealth. Now, it is time I offer the same concepts and advice to you.

What is your story with money? Can you see how it might be harmful? This book provides you with a detailed framework for change, exploring the four levels of Conscious Wealth and serving as a guide for anyone seeking a healthy relationship with their money and investments. I use my own money story—the good, the bad, and the ugly—as an example of how to move through the levels, as well as a model for healing.

The Conscious Wealth mindset is earmarked by levels of Abundance, Purpose, Impact, and Unity. From start to finish, these levels are accessible to all—from those just beginning their journey on wealth creation to the billionaires.

The first level, Abundance, is punctuated by the affirmative statement, "I have enough." You will be asked to look at your limiting, long-held beliefs around money, and come to understand your worthiness in regard to a life filled with an abundance of money, but also resources, relationships, and love. It may require you to define money differently than you were raised to believe.

"I am enough!" is a thread through Purpose, the second level of Conscious Wealth. Here, you are encouraged to define your purpose and spend your money in ways that bring out your truest self, as well as checking your direction once you are committed to a path toward wealth creation. You are also asked to face your demons when it comes to scarcity fears, because once past that, you are able to heal your relationship with your work, family, and business—much of what may have been neglected or misdirected in your quest for financial wealth.

The third level is Impact, where you are asked to consider your choices, understand the financial services you are using, and the change you can bring about in business, including challenging your own company and your industry to do better. The purpose of wealth management is not simply to make money, but also to support individuals and families to become more loving and generous human beings, and actively reduce the conditions that lead to fear, scarcity, and hoarding.

The final level of Conscious Wealth, Unity, is aspirational, questioning individuality and universal connection. You'll learn to empower yourself, your children, and, at the same time, the children of a parent across the world. There are profound implications around how you are in the world, and how you spend and "give" your money away. The ultimate healing here is when you begin to return the excess power and money you have accumulated during wealth creation. Only by letting it go, can you grow in this level.

As I've said, Conscious Wealth provided me a framework to begin my own healing around money. I had destroyed so much in my quest for riches, but am now enjoying a higher state of living. There are moments I still have fear and am selfish, but, because of the solid structure I have created for my work and relationships, those negative moments are the exception.

Since readjusting my life to live based on this concept, I now get the first call when a client is sick, in a car accident, checking into rehab, or even getting a divorce. That might not sound super pleasant or even positive, yet it is an honor to be that trusted as an advisor.

I invite you to journey along with me, the guy who had it all and had absolutely nothing to show for it. The guy who transformed that experience into a life filled with abundance, purpose, impact, and unity with the bigger world, respecting the connections I am making along the way.

It's time to change your narrative around money. To change the definition of *more*. And you are the person for the job.

# LEVEL ONE

# ABUNDANCE

# CHAPTER 1
# AM I WORTH IT?

**Money is a source of deep unease for many,** even for those who have boatloads. I grew up with three siblings in Cleveland, where my parents owned a deli but not much else; I definitely understand financial insecurity and wanting to make "enough" money. However, the truth is, there is never enough money and being "financially successful" cannot make you emotionally or spiritually whole. That kind of happiness is only achieved if you understand your relationship with money and the wider world.

*Conscious Wealth* is a philosophy about wealth and connection on all levels, including the idea that it is okay for you to have money and to spend it. Conscious Wealth also provides a way to think about your wealth, which includes recognizing how you are worthy of all the universe's abundances; how best to use it to bring your truest self to fruition as you develop your purpose; how you can help to bring the best version of our communities and the greater world to fruition, making positive impacts with your money; and how you can reach a state of oneness with every being in the universe.

And let's be clear: Conscious Wealth is not about being like Richie Rich. "Rich" people have everything and still obsess about dumb things like taxes, they always want more, and have the desire to show everybody how rich they are. They are rich but live in scarcity. Wealthy people, on the other hand, are settled, grounded, count family as part of their wealth, don't like paying taxes but understand it is their unwanted responsibility, are immensely grateful, don't see themselves as more or less wealthy than others, and find ways to use their money to help others.

To get to a place where you are healing around money and making choices based on the principles of Conscious Wealth and moving within the financial framework detailed in these pages, we are going to explore the four levels of development, which I call Abundance, Purpose, Impact, and Unity.

# THE THEORY OF ABUNDANCE

In order to really get the concept of Conscious Wealth, you must first embrace a truth that is hard for many of us to believe: there is an abundance of love, friendship, opportunities, resources, and wealth available to you *right now*.

**You just have to find a way to see yourself as worthy and then choose to move forward with confidence, believing that the universe will provide if you open yourself up to it. Easy, right?**

I know from firsthand experience that getting to a place where you feel worthy of abundance, whether trying to achieve it or to keep it, requires a mind shift. All of us are dealing with insecurity at some level. But we can't let it get in the way! You can choose to live in the negative, constantly stressed over scarcity, or you can choose to recognize there are problems but adopt the abundance mentality; meaning, your decisions, or indecisions, are not coming from a place of fear. This is the first step to acquiring the wealth that is already around you, just outside your perception, allowing you to also embrace Conscious Wealth practices.

Let's start by taking a hard look at what I call my *Money Memory* and how it was shaped, including how any feelings of unworthiness may have come into being.

After reading my story, please consider the following questions: How do *you* spend money? How do you earn it, how do you save it, and how do you give it away? Evaluating this highlight reel of your lifetime of experiences or interactions with money will reveal your Money Memory. Let's dig in.

## MONEY MEMORY: THE PAST

As a twenty-year-old student at the Miami University of Ohio, the trajectory of my life was traumatically changed with one horrifying phone call.

On that day, what was to be the shittiest day of my life, I happened to be attending a board meeting for our Catholic Parish, where I was an active catechist for high school students. It had started out great; much to my surprise, the board nominated me as chair. I was flattered by the gesture, too young to realize no one else wanted the position.

In the muggy church basement, basking in my glory, I leaned back in my chair and grinned. Then, the leader of the high school Catechism program interrupted my thoughts, leaning down to whisper, "You have a phone call, Brandon. Please take it in my office."

It was my parents on the line.

They told me how my mother had found my older brother laying on the floor of their garage, dead. Carbon monoxide poisoning. He was on the floor instead of inside the car because, apparently, he'd had a change of heart and tried to escape back to life. He was twenty-one.

I was so confused. My parents kept asking how I felt, seemingly more concerned about me than my brother! "Brandon are you okay?" they asked repeatedly. I wanted to say, "No, are you?" But I didn't. It was unsettling. They sounded as if they had already processed the loss of their son and come to terms with his death even though it had just happened. It was as if they told themselves, "We're going to call Brandon, be very strong, and make sure he doesn't feel bad about this." Their response felt so off, so . . . weird.

I put down the phone. I left and drove off into the woods, spending hours among the trees, my mind flipping around and around, never able to hold onto any one thought for long. I kept thinking, *This is no big deal, this is no big deal . . . Wait . . . Why don't I feel anything?* Eventually, I returned home to find my friends worried sick, concerned about my emotional state and how I'd just disappeared after hearing bad news. Their concerns never crossed my mind. Neither did it occur me to go back to my parents' home that night. It wasn't just that it was a five-hour drive; it was because I couldn't think of anything—anyone—not even myself. I was stuck, too much in shock to move forward.

But the decision was made for me. My brother-in-law picked me up and drove me home. The saddest U2 songs in existence, like *Streets Have No Name* and *With Or Without You*, blared from the CD player. I hated him for it, and I hated U2.

It is rumored that one time Bono was in a concert in Brazil and his percussion guy was striking the drum with the foot pedal like a heartbeat. With each thud, Bono tapped his boot dramatically on the stage. The crowd came to near silence. Every time his foot hit the ground, Bono declared another kid had just died a senseless death of malaria, tuberculosis, or some other sinister disease in Africa. After about twenty foot taps, a guy in the fifth row broke the silence and screamed in Portuguese, "Stop! Stop tapping your foot, you son of a b—!" To this day, it is one of my favorite stories in which causation and correlation are confused. The foot tapping had become too painful to bear, even though it was really the emotional toll of the stories weighing down the audience. Similarly, I'd felt a raging hatred for U2 in my brother-in-law's car, but it was really a raging hatred for the uncontrollable swell of emotions and family memories stabbing at my heart.

For a long time afterward, people would ask, almost daily, "Why did he do it?" I didn't know. "Was there a note?" Yes. "Did it say anything?" Not really. "Was he depressed?" Duh! My brother killed himself for a thousand reasons and, yet, we will never know which one it was. This is just how depression works.

My family was devastated, and I was simply numb. Sadly, I held onto the numbness for a decade. My brother's death created a hole in my life that can never be filled. To me, losing a brother felt like it was right up there with losing a child.

I walked around in a fog the first few days. I know now that fog is called grief. My dad coped by taking sedatives. My childhood friend flew in from California for the service but I didn't have it in me to talk to him. One of my brother's friends dealt with his grief by slipping a joint into the casket, out of love. I guess that is what potheads do at funerals.

I did not look in the casket. I have always been a visual person and wanted to self-select the last image of my older brother.

The first day after the wake—I think it lasted two days—I stood in the doorway of my parents' room. My mother was sitting on the edge of her bed, opening a small stack of envelopes, each filled with cash. I watched her carefully read the notes attached to the monetary tokens as tears cascaded down her face. She sobbed a mixture of gratitude and sadness.

I did not feel the same way. In fact, I was pissed.

The money was from family and friends. They knew how expensive services could be and how we as a family were ill-prepared for a huge financial burden like this.

I was angry we did not have enough money to bury my brother. I am not sure if this was a truth—but that was my interpretation. I had good reason to believe this: I'd grown up wearing hand-me-downs, pants with holes in the knees. Now, I felt disgusted. I'd grown up in a household where I knew my mom felt powerless to the whims of the family business, a deli that my dad controlled. That powerlessness trickled down. I'd felt utterly powerless my entire life, knowing we did not have enough money for emergencies. Now, on top of that, I knew my family was not in any *emotional* shape to handle this tragedy.

In a very foolish and brave gesture, I decided at that moment I would be the rock. I would bring my family through the ordeal.

That moment, in my parents' bedroom doorway, is where my Money Memory started to take its current shape.

As a traumatized twenty-year-old, I turned around and stomped off so I wouldn't have to watch my mom gratefully open up those packets of other people's money. How was it that we were still so poor after all these years that we couldn't even take care of my brother's funeral? Maybe I was projecting my rage at his suicide onto our money situation, but I think that anger had already been there a long time, buried.

Like anyone who faces an unimaginable loss, I eventually got to the point that the grief was manageable. However, some real scars had formed. I'd tried to just "get over it," but I wasn't able to put it behind me. I did have plenty of fun and adventure in my twenties and thirties, but there was always a layer of sadness clinging to me. I thought I was doing a great job hiding it, but I'm pretty sure everybody knew I wasn't happy.

In my thirties, I signed up for sessions with a life coach to help me with my career. The night before my first appointment, though, I had a dream about my brother and was shaken up. I called the life coach and told her we might need to call in some heavier hitters. I ended up with a licensed therapist, knowing I had a lot of work to do. Within three sessions with her, I was liberated from the shame that haunted me for seventeen years, especially after I went home and wrote a letter to my brother. I apologized for any wrongs I committed and told him I regretted his decision. The letter also explained that his decisions were his own and that I would no longer hold myself responsible for them. I showed the letter to my therapist, and she started to cry. Now, that is when you know you are in deep—when your therapist cries.

After a few short months, I did what the Persian poet Rumi advocates in his poem: "Your task is not to seek for love, but merely to seek and find all the barriers within yourself that you have built against it."

What does this have to do with Money Memory? Or Bono tapping his foot?

As I grew up, I created a lot of false truths that seemingly correlated, but really had nothing to do with one another. I believed if I worried about money, I wouldn't have to worry about money. I believed that if I didn't have the money for something, I did not "need" it. And I believed, at times, that because my brother was no longer here, I should no longer be at ease with joy in the world. These beliefs actually served me well at the time and allowed me to deal with the experiences I was given.

**The name of the game was survival and I survived. But, then, I reached the point when I needed to question those beliefs in order to *go beyond just survival.***

Can you imagine if I'd been an impetuous kid, nagging my parents for fresh basil and a block of parmesan at the dinner table? No, back then, in survival mode, we were happy to have Ragu and a green tube of Kraft Cheese with our spaghetti noodles. But later, when I could afford finer foods, foods that I enjoyed, why was I still avoiding them?

I grew up in a frugal household in the eighties, where leather interior in a car was considered outlandish and frivolous. Like I said earlier, I rarely had a new pair of pants, not to mention ones without holes in the knees. Even as a kid, I perpetually stressed over poverty. I was constantly afraid that one wrong step would make my family homeless. One year, I remember feeling horrible about how much my parents spent on Christmas gifts. I opened my presents with dread, afraid that the holiday ritual would put my family on the street.

On top of that, I was afraid I would have to tell a lie about liking a present on that sacred day, knowing I'd feel terrible if my parents had spent hard-earned money on something I did not like. To this day, I still get a little uncomfortable with the ubiquitous expression of joy around the Christmas season. Money Memory is sticky.

As an adult, even after I was earning good money, when I was doing well in my career, I was stingy, sure that it could evaporate at any minute and I would be left destitute and filled with shame again. I had built very strong barriers against abundance, because I was sure it was never going to happen for me. Or, if it did, I wouldn't deserve it.

# MONEY MEMORY: THE PRESENT

By confronting my sense of survivor's guilt around my brother's choices, I opened myself up to a more fulfilling life. This was a life abundant with meaningful relationships, work, and endeavors. The dreams stopped, the guilt subsided, and I began to thrive.

Now it was time to challenge my Money Memory. I needed to rewrite my money story.

To celebrate, I made a bucket list. I still find it kind of weird for somebody in their thirties to make a bucket list, but I did it anyway. One of the items on the list was to buy a *really* expensive bottle of wine. The price tag had to be over two hundred dollars; I picked that number because I thought it was a ridiculous amount of money for wine. I had some additional stipulations. First of all, the bottle had to come from a store. It couldn't be some marked-up bottle at a restaurant. Second, it could not be paid for by a corporate expense account. The money had to come from me and me alone.

No matter how I looked at it, two hundred dollars for a bottle of wine seemed bananas to me at the time. Yeah, I get the law of supply and demand, but that's fifty dollars a glass! Do you know what I could do with fifty bucks? I could go to my favorite neighborhood bar, buy some wings, have a cold beer, and still have change in my pocket. I could get authentic Indian food at a local restaurant at least twice. I could buy three bottles of my usual wine. Or, in this case, I could buy one measly glass.

But there was a purpose to this project.

## I wanted to prove a point to myself. I needed to separate myself and my future from the Money Memory of my past.

Months after my breakthrough with the therapist, I found the perfect two-hundred-dollar bottle of wine. I was ready to prove my Money Memory wrong. I wanted to prove to myself I am worthy of a vintage bottle most people wouldn't even consider buying. Instead of writing affirmations on my bathroom mirror and repeating them every morning like Stuart Smalley, I chose to live by the credo "Actions speak louder than words." And, so, I bought that damn bottle of wine.

I drank the bottle of Cos D'Estournel 2004 with a friend on a snowy Tuesday afternoon when the city of Atlanta was shut down by two inches of snow. Not a typo—two inches. I savored every sip. This wine had sat in oak for two years before bottling. Then it sat for another ten before I uncorked it. Noticeably toasty, oaky, earthy, with many layers of vanilla and other flavors I couldn't put my finger on, it was the best wine I have ever had. But to be fair, most wines

I'd purchased were from a grocery store and had pictures of safari animals on the label. Truly, though, this wine was luscious. It was a gift to myself. It was a message: I was worth it. No pairing with a celebration or meal. No figs or moldy cheese. Just a bottle of Cos D'Estournel between friends. It took us eight hours to drink that wine, with a nap in the middle. And as I drank each glass, sip by sip, the taste transformed and became more profound throughout the day.

## AVOIDING EXTREMES

Part of my journey was to recognize that I am worthy of the finer things in life and that it was not superfluous or silly to spend money on myself. Somewhere in years of scrimping and saving to make ends meet, the wires got crossed and the message distorted. That message said I was not *worth* the finer things in life, when, in fact, the true message was I thought I could not *afford* the finer things in life. That bottle of wine, and all the joy that came with it, was priceless. With each sip of wine, my Money Memory was also transformed. Not erased, not forgotten, just transformed with new experiences and memories.

That is what is interesting about our Money Memories: the same exact experience can push different people to different extremes. My Money Memory from my younger years pushed me to frugality. It did not have to be that way. I could have just as easily been moved to be extravagant. I could have spent every dime I had on the most luxurious things. I had enough money and credit, I could have drunk Dom every night, lived in a five-thousand-square-foot penthouse apartment, and leased a yellow Lambo. My frugal upbringing and embarrassment over my family's perceived inability to afford to bury my brother could have led me to that extravagance. Thankfully, I found a balance as I asked questions and explored my beliefs.

Intense frugality and extreme extravagance—neither extremes are desirable in the long term. Money Memories take different journeys, but extreme spending habits often start in the same place: a place of shame, embarrassment, or unworthiness.

As I worked through my story, I found a place on the spectrum between extravagance and frugality that fit with my current situation. I continuously check in with my beliefs and see how they mesh with who I am right now. As you write your story, the same can happen for you.

## YOU ARE WORTHY

For a long time, it was important for me to claim, "I don't live extravagantly." I wouldn't want anyone to think I was uppity or even living beyond my means, right? *But why should I care what others thought?* It all had to do with my own perceptions of myself, of my Money Memory.

I have created hundreds of financial plans over the years and this issue with perceived "extravagance" is a common thread with my clients. Families with completely different budgets will tell me they don't live extravagantly. For sure, they are not lying to me.

Perhaps it's just that everybody believes they don't live extravagantly, because they are using different reference points, such as comparing themselves to the Joneses, the Kardashians, or some form of publicized excess that implicitly gives us permission to be just slightly less ostentatious. Rich is always ten million dollars more than you have. If you have nothing, somebody with ten million dollars is rich. If you have ten million dollars, you look up the ladder and think, *That guy with twenty million dollars is rich.*

My friend pointed out that the happiest people describe their spending in what they actually do, not what they don't do. This makes sense to me. *Just own it.* Heck, I live in a premier neighborhood in Atlanta, eat out more than once a week (pre-COVID), drink wine more nights than not—although not the two-hundred-dollar-a-bottle variety—and go on a two-week international vacation every year. I live extravagantly, if by no other measure, than compared to the lifestyle I grew up with. And I am immensely grateful for it.

Some five years after the glorious day with the bottle of wine, I went to the office like any other day and went about my work. That midafternoon, a lady from the skyscraper next to my building jumped off the balcony to her death. Yes, life is not all that it seems in the affluent Atlanta neighborhood of Buckhead. Buckhead has the reputation, whether it deserves it or not, as the elitist part of town. A quick glance out my window will spot you a Dior, Tom Ford, and Hermes store. The office was pretty shaken up, and, for a second, I tried to remain blasé. I caught myself burying the emotions around her suicide, so I consciously forced myself to be in the moment and deal with my feelings.

I sat still for a few moments and scanned my body for discomfort. I felt sadness—profound sadness—but this time I did not feel shame.

I did not feel unworthiness for my beautiful office, my productive profession, or all the other fortunate things in my life. I allowed myself to feel that sadness, because I am now wise enough to know it needs to be recognized. After a few minutes, I got back to work. It was only later that night on Facebook that I realized this was the anniversary of my brother's death and thought, *Holy shit, this world works in really strange ways.*

Years after my two-hundred-dollar bottle of wine, I fell in love and began a long-term partnership with my girlfriend. I quickly learned that not everybody likes washing dishes by hand or heating up coffee in a wok—the only pan in my bachelor studio. Most people don't want their towels to dry and exfoliate them at the same time. Some people like owning nice wine glasses. Others actually like different wine glasses for different types of wine. Who knew? The list of the few possessions I thought I could get by with has now expanded. In most ways, it has been nice. I enjoy having nicer things—but I am glad my partner and I both agree that they are just things.

So, we live our lives. Me without my burden of survivor's guilt after the loss of my brother or the negative narrative I had adopted around my family's issues with money. I'd overcome the underlying thorny belief that because I was *abandoned* by my brother, that, somehow, I was not worthy of finer things. Yes, I know, those two things obviously have no correlation . . . but the stories we develop of ourselves don't always make sense. Just as Bono was not killing a starving kid in Africa by tapping his toe, I was not abandoned by my brother. He abandoned *life* because it was too hard for him. His death wasn't about me. To boot, it's not that I was unworthy of the finer things in life, it's just that we did not have the money for them. It's not like my parents made me wear corduroys with holes in the knees because that's all I was worth to them.

Rewriting your story is no small feat. But by doing so, you can transform how you think. How you process your issues around money. It took time, presence, courage, and in my case, some assistance from professional therapists. I unknowingly echoed Rilke's advice to a young artist when he said, "And the point is, to live everything. Live the questions now. Perhaps you will then gradually, without noticing it, live along some distant day into the answer."

Today, it is no longer about whether I am worthy of the finer things in life. I can pay for things and experiences that I want but don't need. At the same time, I do not have to buy everything I want or can afford. I can continue to consciously shape my Money Memory with a clearer mind and open heart because *I alone am enough*.

*I am worth it.*

Reshaping your Money Memory is the first step toward Conscious Wealth. Once you determine you are worth it, your journey can begin. We all have money beliefs. If the negative ones go unnoticed, they start to creep into our lives and wreak havoc. In order to move forward, they must be confronted, examined, scrutinized, and accepted.

# YOUR STORY

I encourage you to write your own story. The only thing worse than spending your entire life drinking ten-dollar bottles of wine because you don't believe you deserve better is spending your life drinking two-hundred-dollar bottles of wine and not truly enjoying them.

Writing your money story can help heal your issues with the past.

Here are some questions to get you started. I encourage you to write out the answers. Discuss with friends and family members. Really process and explore. Go deep.

* What is your earliest memory about money?
* What emotions surface when you think about money?
* Think of a time you were overly frugal. Think of a time when you overspent. What were the circumstances around those two scenarios? Do you see any similarities?
* Are you overspending out of feelings of worthiness or unworthiness? Where are you underspending? Is it out of feelings of worthiness or unworthiness?
* What would your Money Memory timeline look like? Want to make this really meaningful? I suggest you buy a roll of blank paper, rip off a ten-foot segment, and attach the banner to your wall. On the far left side, write BIRTH. On the far right, PRESENT DAY. Label certain years or big experiences as markers, if you like. Then, write down all the experiences you've ever had with money that you can remember.

The first time the tooth fairy gave you a quarter, how it made you feel, and what you did with it. Same with your first allowance. The first time you had to pay someone back. Your first paycheck. Your first parking fine. Your first lottery ticket. The first time you used a credit card. By doing this, you will see patterns in regards to how you felt about money at certain points in your life.

# CHAPTER 2
# WHO AM I?

Pioneer photojournalist Robert Capa said, "If your pictures aren't good enough, then you're not close enough."

The same can be said for Conscious Wealth.

**If you have enough money and yet you don't feel good enough, then you're not close enough . . . you're not close enough to your family, friends, coworkers, stakeholders, or even the security guard who greets you at the door each morning.**

If you have plenty of money but find that you are using more energy preserving and protecting possessions or the trappings of wealth (personal assistants, multiple cars, gated communities) instead of preserving your personal relationships, you are likely unhappy. You are not close enough because your money is getting in the way, it is between you and what matters, instead of being used as a tool to draw you closer. If you have lost sight of the abundance around you, you are not truly wealthy.

Admittedly, it can be a challenge to switch to the

abundance mindset. One important element of doing so is to figure out who you are and who you want to be. Easy, right?

# ADVENTURE AS SELF-DISCOVERY

My family argued so much that I moved to a different continent to get away from them. It is not that I did not like my family. They just loved to get to the bottom of things. All the time. It has been like that my whole life—we argued on family vacations, when trying to get to church on time, or at the dinner table. I took on the full-time position of peacekeeper. It was exhausting. That is one reason why, a mere seven days after college, I left the country. It was a welcome break from the tension and drama of living in a big family. And I wanted to see who I could be without them.

My first job out of college was working on cruise ships as a youth activities director for a few years. It was awesome. Here I was, a "poor" kid from Cleveland on a cruise ship, seeing the world and getting paid for it. It may be hard to believe, but I had never had sushi, salmon, duck, and certainly not caviar or even espresso before being on those ships. I had never left the United States, except to see Niagara Falls. With this new job, I was in a new country every port of call. It was a far cry from my upbringing.

Not only did my international employment open my eyes to the immense variety of food in the world, it also provided me exceptional exposure to diversity as well. Cruise ships may be the most diverse collection of human beings in a defined space at a single time. A crew of different ages, different races, sexual orientation, different family dynamics, beliefs, and motivations are all cloistered together on a floating vessel for a few months at a time. In order for me to schedule a pool party for our young passengers, I had to engage a Dutch, a Filipino, an Indonesian, and an American to schedule the pool, food, linen distribution, and venue. For each person I spoke with, I had to conduct myself differently—according to their customs and culture. Occasionally, my written schedule would literally say "schmooze," which meant I had to wander the ship and buy people drinks.

It was a great gig, but it was not enough. It was fun to travel the Caribbean, Alaska, and Europe, but after a few years, I grew tired of visiting. I wanted to live somewhere and sink my teeth into the culture.

I decided I would use my college degree and teach history overseas. I called one of the two international school recruiters (yes, at the time there were only two) and told them I wanted to work at an international school and put my degree to good use. He said I needed two years of experience to even be considered for a job. Then I made him an offer he couldn't refuse.

"Have you ever had anyone back out of teaching contracts at the last minute?" I asked.

"Yes, that has happened once or twice."

"How much does that suck? Look, the next time that happens, you give me a call. I will go anywhere in the world, teach at any school. I need a minimum of five days' notice."

I finished my cruise contract that summer, but then

the cruise line called and offered me the 90-Day World Cruise. Yes, normally, I would have jumped at a world tour. But, instead, I said, "Thanks, but I am going to stay around here and try for something that challenges me. I'm not sure what that might be, but I'll figure it out." The company called me back in an hour; the rep exclaimed, "Brandon, I'm perplexed! I just offered you the world, and you said no." I laughed because that was one heck of a flattering hard sell.

True to my word, I waited for something better—and, a few weeks later, I got it.

The recruiter called to let me know some guy had broken his teaching contract prematurely. I jumped on the opportunity to start at a new school in Egypt with a handful of others. As I hung up the phone, I smiled from ear to ear, shouting, "I'm moving to Egypt!"

I was ready for the adventure. And more than ready to do something meaningful with my time and talents. I would be a good teacher, and maybe even make the world a better place. I knew myself well enough to know I had more to offer than coordinating kids' pool parties.

Yes, I was idealistic. But I was following my heart. I was going to be making far less money as a teacher than I had working on the cruise ships, and I could not care less. And I was right to think that while I was overseas, the lack of money didn't bother me. I have never been happier.

In hindsight, however, it is clear that while I was following up on my passions for adventure and teaching, I was also running away from money. One reason I was happy was because I was avoiding money and all the traumatic memories or decisions it can bring with it.

# FOLLOWING PASSION INSTEAD OF WEALTH

Nine days later, there I was, twenty-four years old, teaching history in Egypt.

It was an adventure from the start. I must've looked the quintessential tourist. The day I landed, I couldn't keep a grin off my face. The dust in the air, the chaotic traffic, the crowded market I wandered through without knowing a lick of Arabic . . . I was enchanted, deeply in love with the place. For a short while, anyway.

Since I was replacing someone who'd abruptly broke their contract, I had less than a week's notice before I taught my first class. I was working in one of the premier neighborhoods, teaching Egyptian children in upper-middle-class families, so the bar was high. Yet, I had to figure out how to create and implement curriculum at the same time I was trying to figure out how to buy bread and turn on my shower.

I quickly learned that even with all my experience traveling on ships with tourists from around the globe, I was not prepared for so many new experiences occurring simultaneously. It was my first time living overseas, my first teaching job with students whose native language was not English, and I was living in an apartment alone for the first time. The intense culture shock was a surprising slap upside the head.

For example, simply going to the grocery store was a challenge. The neighborhood stores were like old-fashioned bodegas with one long counter, straight out of the 1950s. If you wanted something, you had to ask the clerk for it in Arabic, so I would have to use my dictionary to write a shopping list before leaving my apartment. Once the clerk finally understood me, he'd grab the item from under the counter or from shelves along the wall behind him. Then, you were expected to haggle over the price. Just getting a container of yogurt was exhausting.

It was frustrating at times, but I really *lived* when I was there. I saw the opera *Aida* at the base of the pyramids, I went scuba diving in the Red Sea, and I took a train to Alexandria and traveled to the Oases near the Libyan border. Using a tip I'd learned from a John Travolta film I'd seen as a kid, where he showered in his clothes so he could wash them and himself at the same time, I was able to backpack around southern Egypt and live off two or three changes of clothes for weeks. It was raw, bohemian, highly stressful, and exciting.

And because I was still learning to really listen to others, one of the most embarrassing moments of my life happened while I was there. I had been swimming laps in a public pool when a man approached and said something in Arabic. Realizing I didn't know what he was saying, he switched to English.

"Not polite to swim in front of woman."

"But we're in a pool and people swim together," I protested, waving my arm at the other men and women. He repeated himself but I insisted I was there to swim and swim I would. I wasn't offending anyone. But, well . . . I was. He gestured with his hands, using charades to tell me something was wrong with my shorts. Too short, maybe? They looked fine to me.

"Mister, your ass is showing," he finally said.

It was. Every time I'd performed a flip turn, I was

mooning a poor woman in a hijab sitting on the side. What must have started as a small tear had become a wide-open flap from the waist down, thanks to all those turns. I turned beet red as I looked up at the woman. Her hand was tucked under the fabric of the hijab, covering her mouth as she giggled. The Egyptians had such a great sense of humor. Luckily.

Egypt was often like an adrenaline-filled adventure movie, though with no romantic twist or ending in sight. On my way to work, I would cross the Nile and walk polluted streets so entrenched with poverty it was almost unbearable. Growing up, I'd witnessed homelessness in downtown Cleveland. My dad was always chasing away beggars, hookers, and johns from the corner of 36th and Euclid, where he had his restaurant. But I had never seen impoverishment like this before.

Even though it bothered me, I finally had to make peace with it. Perhaps out of necessity. I mean, I couldn't be a blathering mess every time I left my apartment and my eyes landed on a beggar. But it was not acceptance. The knowledge of what I was witnessing gave my work meaning.

Here I was, in one of the poorest countries in the world, teaching the Egyptian children from the upper economic class families, and empowering them to learn compassion and perspective. I knew that if I could teach them those skills, it would have a ripple effect on society. That epiphany changed something in me.

I took this experience in Egypt and drew upon it. When my contract was up, I moved on to teach the children of wealthy nationals (diplomats and executives at multinational companies) in Lebanon and Brazil.

I provided my students with an insight into issues of human rights, public safety, and justice. All the while, I was growing as a human being, traveling the world and meeting new people.

I didn't make a lot of money at the time, but I loved my work.

I had purpose.

## USING PASSION TO FIND ENRICHMENT

Early on, I returned to the US to visit my parents and bought a camera.

I soon discovered that my camera didn't just provide me with cool photos: it provided me with armor. To combat the stress of Egypt's darker realities and the culture shock, I took refuge behind the lens. That camera allowed me to be a vigilant observer and capture my experiences, but, if I'm being honest, it also became my security blanket.

Initially, I brought the camera back with me to take black-and-white photos, which I thought would be as cool and dramatic as my life felt. I had been looking at photos of Cartier-Bressen, Capa, and the Magnum greats. And, so, I took to the streets. I captured images between bites of braised pigeon while perched on restaurant balconies or hidden behind sacks of flour in the market. The photos were raw, and the experience for me was fascinating. I shot roll after roll with a telephoto lens, learning about Egyptian culture from afar while training my eye, pleased with how my new camera enhanced my life.

A year later, when I took a teaching assignment in Lebanon, I made friends with Ben, a seasoned photographer. He was the one who schooled me about "stealing photos," which is what they called it when you take photos of people without them knowing.

One day, we approached a village in the Bekaa Valley; I saw a group of Bedouin walking in our direction. I put on my telephoto lens and starting shooting. Ben appeared in my viewfinder, blocking my shot as he approached my subjects—"stolen" subjects, he explained later. *Damnit!* I thought. *He is ruining the moment.* A real and natural photo, in my mind, was one that is not known to the subject. Otherwise, I believed, the subject was just posing, creating an emotion for the moment.

Ben, on the other hand, was greeting those he wanted to photograph and carrying on conversations. And as they spoke, he began to take photos. He'd lift his camera, take a few clicks, and then lower it to ask a question. As the Bedouin responded, he'd sneak in a few more clicks. And on and on it went. The more they interacted, the more all parties became relaxed. For the subjects of the photo, the camera was forgotten. For the photographer, it became a mere extension of his eye, and he naturally and effortlessly took photos. It punctuated sentences. It filled voids. It brought complete strangers together in an engaging exchange of ideas.

Soon, I was inside a Bedouin tent drinking tea and being offered daughters' hands in marriage. I knew after spending my first day with Ben, this was *the* way to capture photos.

What I didn't know at the time, partly because I was undergoing a deep, personal growth phase and recovering from culture shock, was this: by crouching behind a sack of flour in Egypt, I was isolating myself and projecting what I thought was important about an outside culture. What protected me, disconnected me from the people. And blocked me from the depths of passion I could have been achieving.

Although the camera helped me grow my knowledge base and provided a good training ground for me to conquer photographic techniques, it hardly left me fulfilled. If I'd kept on this track, I would have mastered photography and probably grown bored with it, moving on to the next shiny thing.

Ben didn't see the camera as protection. He saw it as a bridge to human connection. From that day on, my camera was firmly established as a pathway to seeing beyond myself. As a hobbyist, I embraced photography because it was a tool for meeting people and discovering the foreign cultures of Egypt, Lebanon, and Brazil.

I carried these lessons to my next teaching assignment in Brazil. My passion for photography offered me a connection to the place and the people I never thought possible.

I followed religious pilgrims around the northeast of Brazil and interviewed them while clicking away. They were there to honor the late Padre Cicero, an excommunicated priest who was seen as the people's "saint" in a small, isolated village in the northeast of Brazil. As I snapped away, I asked them one question: "Who is Padre Cicero?" Oftentimes, their response was as much a reflection of themselves as Padre Cicero.

I recorded the answer and paired them with the photos.

Most of the time, though, I took to the streets with no agenda. Spontaneous discoveries often yielded the strongest and most unexpected connections—connections to myself and to complete strangers. No longer a security blanket, photography quickly became my passion and an escape from my growing frustration with teaching, where my idealism was coming up hard against the administration's philosophy of placing the responsibility of learning on the teacher versus the student, while also forcing me to teach more and more classes.

While I loved the kids and believed in what I was doing, teaching in this way was no longer feeding my passion. However, thanks to my experience with Ben and the Bedouins, my camera was no longer an object that simply enhanced my life—photography was a hobby that *enriched* my life. You see, an enhancement is something external added to improve the quality of life. But an *enrichment* improves life through connections with other human beings. Prior to this shift, my photos served a limited purpose in my education and personal growth, since I was behind the camera and purposefully outside the action. Now, my photos represented a relationship I had with others, truly enriching my knowledge by being *in* the world. And I never felt more like myself, or more accepting of that self, than when I had a camera at my eye, interacting with others, and seeing myself as clearly as I saw them.

Capa said we need to get closer. Money can do that, but only if we let it, instead of allowing it to come between us and our relationships with people and experiences.

**Connection to others is necessary to discover who we are and who we could be. We never really understand ourselves in isolation.**

Today, there is an epidemic of people searching outside of themselves for passion and purpose. They are suffering from anxiety as they juggle a world of obligations and desires while striving to live with intent and meaning. I still find myself doing this more often than I'd like to admit.

# WHO AM I WITHOUT MONEY?

Seven years and three countries later, the zeal for teaching eventually dried up. Why? Well, because no one can maintain that level of passion indefinitely—I transitioned to the role of full-time photographer.

Within months, I opened up a studio. I jumped from a clearly defined identity as a teacher with a steady paycheck to a freestyle form of self-discovery. I felt liberated. But that didn't last long. I quickly learned that the "freestyle" approach was actually stressful for me. I needed more structure. Also, it did not lead to profits.

I decided to build a business as a paid photographer. I hired staff and built up a client base. And realized I was still unhappy. There was no longer a sense of enrichment, of being connected to something greater than myself. I was shooting weddings and portraits of pregnant women to pay the bills but had little interest in my subjects' lives. (For one, I was single, saw marriage as a trap, and had little desire to raise my own children.)

So, I then decided to close up shop. It wasn't me.

My work does not define me. It simply reflects who I am. People say the loss of their business is a hard blow to overcome because, along with financial stability, they lose their self-identity. I had a different experience. I did not need to reinvent myself after I walked away from teaching, or even when I closed the photography business. Instead, I chose to learn who I was without my money.

Photography was a passion that added enrichment to my life, and provided ways for me to be artistic and find meaning and connection. But I didn't have to rely on photography as my sole form of fulfillment—I found what I really loved was to learn what drives other people, to fight injustices, and to teach. That is who I am, money or no. But by knowing this about myself, I could create a path forward to a career that would be enriching, would feed my passion, and allow me to be purposeful. By knowing this about myself, I could see a path to a life filled with more connection and abundance.

## YOUR STORY

So, who are *you* without your money? I get it . . . how do you even begin to process a loaded question like that?

Let's start with what you own. Create a balance sheet of your possessions and categorize them as *Enhancement* or *Enrichment*. Remember, an enhancement is something external added to improve the quality of life. Think heated seats in your car with leather interior. An enrichment, however, improves life through connections with other human beings.

I know we are talking about you here, but I think it best to provide a couple of personal examples.

Today, my only car is a 1999 BMW Z3 Coupe. The car is nicknamed the "Clown Shoe" because of its elongated shape. There is no middle ground with this car—you either love it or hate it. I bought the car because it is quirky, sporty, and stylish—all things I like to think about myself. Nevertheless, the car is just an enhancement. It is more fun than driving a Toyota Corolla, but it is really just a car—it doesn't make me a better Brandon.

In contrast, I am a member of a sailing club with annual dues. It provides me the opportunity to sail with people I've come to care about. I spend hours sailing with these friends—which involves raising sails, tacking, or changing directions in the boat and rounding markers—oftentimes in some pretty intense conditions. We are communicating and growing together as we balance the forces of our weight, the wind, waves, the sails, and the boat. After a sail, we sit around and eat grocery store-made turkey sandwiches and drink a few beers together. These connections are irreplicable to me.

Sometimes, though, I do sail alone, with just my handheld VHF radio. There are times the conditions and my experience are not a perfect match and I am scared. Facing that fear within me is one of the most important things I do. It is definitely an enrichment. Sailing makes me feel alive and connected to myself, to nature, and to my friends.

That is who I am without my money. And ironically, my money got me here.

**You really want just enough enhancements to create enrichments. If you don't feel good enough, it is time to take a closer look at how much of your money goes to one versus the other.**

Use your lists from above to consider the following questions, which can help you on your journey to Conscious Wealth:

- What do you spend money on that enhances your life?
- What do you spend money on that enriches your life?
- What do you spend money on that detracts from your life?
- What would you do if your accountant ran away with all your money to a country in South America (besides hunting him down and shaking him by the ankles)? Who would you be?
- Once you've thought about who you'd be without money, what is a passion or hobby you have (or want to have) that could be used as a springboard into something bigger? How might that hobby or passion provide a purpose for you in the world?

# CHAPTER 3
# HOW MUCH IS ENOUGH?

**I'm guessing you've seen the movie *Wall Street*.** The most poignant moment is when Bud Fox screams, "Tell me, Gordon, when does it all end, huh? How many yachts can you water ski behind? How much is enough?"

Achieving the mindset of Conscious Wealth means coming to terms with this question for yourself. The following stories, information, and even a formula can help you find the answer.

## A SCARCITY MENTALITY

As the youngest of a family of six, "abundance" was not something with which we were familiar.

Access to food in the home required a bit of strategy and cunning. We would shop at Zagara's, the local grocery store chain, and leave with a grocery cart packed sky-high with food. My mom would shake her head in dismay at the bags, loaded with the favorites we had pressured her into: Nutter Butters, yogurt with gobs of fruit syrup at the bottom, Hamburger Helper, chicken pot pies, and a large beef pot roast. Inevitably, our groceries topped the hundred-dollar mark. At home, my mother would caution us, "Now remember, this is all the food I am buying until next week."

As the family organizer, it was my job to put the food in the pantry, lining up cans and basically playing a real-life version of Food Tetris. At times, a Twinkie just happened to end up behind the industrial size can of Chef Boyardee Ravioli and went unnoticed for days. Yes, I was hoarding.

By the third day, the stock would start to dwindle. I would wake up early to get the first go at the cereal, only to learn my sister foraged all the raisins out of the box of Raisin Bran. She left us with plain bran. As the week came to a close, I had to get creative. By day seven, I was using Jell-O mix as Kool-Aid and tried to drink it before it got too cold and congealed.

The lowest point I can recall from my scavenger days occurred when I'd sneak into the bathroom and eat Tums, because they kind of looked and tasted like Smarties candy. I've been told that when I was four, I snuck out of my room, climbed onto the bathroom counter, and started downing all the cough syrup and pills in sight. Apparently, I fell to the floor with a loud thud, waking my parents, who sprang into action. My mother says what she remembers from that night is holding my head over the large salad bowl we used to make tabbouleh, feeding me syrup of ipecac until I'd thrown up multiple times. (Sidenote to parents: please give your kids some sweets and lock medicine in your cabinets.)

Obviously, I survived. On Sundays, we would eat as a family in a small cove carved into the wall of our kitchen, at a wobbly Formica table. We'd forsake the beautiful dining room set my parents received as a wedding gift. To this day, I am not sure why we had a dining room set or nice china if we never used it.

(Hmm, just writing this I detect another source of my Money Memory.)

As the smell of pot roast began to emanate throughout the house, us kids would make our rounds through the kitchen, brimming with anticipation. My mom would call for us to wash our hands and I swear I could faintly hear the sound of first call at a horse track. We clambered to get ready, say the prayer, and push my mother along through the special intentions and requests as she seemingly mentioned everybody she ever met in her entire life, until dinner was finally served. One of my siblings would inevitably whine about how "he got more than me." But I knew better than to complain. I had a job to do.

That job was to appear as calm as possible as I ate swiftly, but not so swiftly I would be chided. The moment the last bite on my plate was in my mouth, I went in for seconds. Oftentimes, I overate just so I wouldn't risk ending the meal feeling hungry.

As a child, I saw reality as one of scarcity. Now, I know those formative experiences would shape my attitudes in the future. But at the time, my mother's belief that there was plenty of food to go around was true. My parents provided enough food, just not enough of the food I wanted. Yet, my siblings and I adopted the view that there was not enough to go around, and we could go hungry. Therefore, strategy, and, at times treachery, were needed to look out for number one. I mean, really, come on, who eats all the raisins out of Raisin Bran?

My mother had four kids in four years before she broke up with the Vatican and opted for birth control.

I was the last to go to school. I spent that entire year before kindergarten driving around in a Suburban with my mom. This large vehicle was yellow and white, and had two gas tanks. Our friends called it the school bus. I proudly rode shotgun and sat above everybody else with my elbow out the window or, at times, with my hand in the up/down wavy motion that still fills my heart with joy. We did grocery shopping, went to the garden center, and whatever else we had to do.

The soundtrack of my childhood was hits from the eighties, playing through a radio with a turn dial and push button presets that dragged a needle from one station to the other. I could ask my mother anything and she would give me deadpan answers—despite my age. I always liked this about her. My mother hated sappy love songs. I remember her disdain for one particular song, so I asked her what it was about. I'll be honest: I was mostly curious because I was certain I heard a bad word in the song. It happened to be Hall and Oats—*Rich Girl*. She stated plainly, "It is about a girl whose parents have so much money she never has to work." That started a conversation about a new guy who'd just moved into the neighborhood. Somehow, everybody knew the newbies were fantastically rich. They owned a tanning salon. Go figure—some guys have all the luck.

# BEING POWERLESS

"Are we middle class?" I asked my mom on one of those many car rides. I have no idea why.

"Lately, I'm not sure we are going to make it," she scoffed.

You see, my mom didn't have a voice in the family finances, and my ears were as good as any when she needed to vent from time to time. I really didn't understand what that meant, but I knew it meant we did not have enough money.

"What are you going to do about it?" I asked. "God will provide," she said. My mother seemed to bypass herself and my father as a source of money and went straight to God the Father to provide.

There was a stark division of duties in our household. My father ran the restaurant and was so busy at the restaurant that he was exempt from household duties, which included cooking, mowing the lawn, or getting his own glass of water when thirsty. His hobbies were bargain hunting and picking up "treasures" left on the curb and bringing them home, to my mother's despair. He was squarely in charge of making and "saving" money.

As the restaurant went, so went the family. My mom raised the kids, ran the household, and, as a hobby, she arranged flowers and snuck some of the "treasures" from our basement and placed them on our own curb after my father went to work. Many years later, when we sold my dad's restaurant, it took me days to empty out the basement. He'd gotten wise to my mother's antihoarding techniques and kept the real treasures hidden there. Most notably, I yanked an entire bumper, the grill, and the headlights of a '68 Cadillac Sedan de Ville from the basement treasure trove. I also dumped a case of Billy Beer, the infamous beer produced in 1977 and 1978 (only!) by Jimmy Carter's older brother. Decades later it had gone rancid, as you can imagine.

Personally, it was the powerlessness—not the real

or perceived poverty—that stuck with me. To this day, I really don't know the true depth of our family money problems back then. My mom now tells me there were months we didn't know where the next mortgage payment was coming from. Later, in my teen years, I suspected much of the hand wringing and "money doesn't grow on trees" talk was a heavy-handed way to have us turn off lights and chew our food slowly.

Yet, despite the overt threat of impending financial doom, my parents insisted I attend one of the top high schools in Cleveland (it was an all-boys Jesuit Catholic school, elite to some, but pragmatic to us), even though it cost nearly the same as a state college at the time. Still does, actually. Remarkably, my mom was able to return the financial aid check my senior year because she got a raise at work. I remember one of the theology teachers coming up to me in the hall and saying it was the first time ever that anybody returned financial aid. I explained to him that my mom believed God provided her with a raise and it was just not right to keep the money when there were people in more need than us. How could a theology teacher argue with that?

While her philosophy may have been true, I assure you, there were people with less financial need than us who were still taking the cash. Honestly, it didn't bother me that we needed aid—almost all my friends from my side of town needed help. I just knew I wasn't going to count on God alone to be my accountant when I grew up. I respected my mom's beliefs, but I didn't quite understand the rationale behind them.

I had someone else in mind when it came to a financial role model.

Every other Christmas, my uncle came over from Chicago in a really cool Chevy StarCraft van—you know, the one with plush club seats and a bed in the back. I would say, "Mom, I want a car like that."

She told me it wasn't my uncle's, but rather, a company car he was using.

"If you want a car like that, you should be an accountant."

That stuck with me.

Eight years later, I registered for Miami University as a business major—Accounting. I entered with an enthusiasm to make money, fueled by a strong sense of scarcity. I did not last long.

I hated accounting and did not like the business world, not back then; it seemed so crass and devoid of meaning. I started studying history and ended up with a degree in secondary education with hours of history and political science courses. I loved it. It was what I needed at the time. I eventually came full circle, though, finding my way back to the business world.

As you know, today I work in wealth management, but it was a long road to this point. After teaching for a number of years, I was deeply entrenched in the scarcity mentality and that didn't change just because I found my way into financial services.

# FEAR-BASED DECISIONS

When I started in the business as a financial advisor, we were trained to ask our prospective clients, "What keeps you up at night?" At the time, it seemed like something logical to ask. But looking back at it now, I realize we were asking them to state their fears. A relationship that begins with, and is based, on fear is not sustainable. Who starts a first date asking, "What is your biggest fear about what will happen in the next two hours?" Or, "What is your biggest fear about dating in your thirties?"

As investment professionals, we were trained—yes, trained—to drum up fears. Perhaps worse, I suspect that many practitioners keep the fear going in order to maintain their clients and use sophisticated financial products to distance them from their money. Is it any wonder many clients change advisors once they realize those fears have yet to be alleviated?

I may not be using fear-based language with clients anymore, but most of them bring their own fears to the table without prompting. I'm not mocking people for being leery regarding their financial future, there is a lot to be afraid of out there. And we're trained to think this way. Besides, it's common sense to manage our money with an eye on the future. But clients often ask the wrong questions in this regard . . . The number one question I get from new clients is, "What is my number?" This means "How much money do I need to store up in the bank so I can live some version of the American dream?" You know—riding off into the sunset, sailing around the world, watching cable news from a recliner, visiting national parks in an RV, planting a garden, and never having to worry about another thing ever again. The problem? These dreams are pretty elusive and that number is different for everybody.

Let's start with the obstacles. The answer to how much is enough for most Americans is a heck of a lot more than what they have right now. It's sad that 19 percent of Americans currently have less than $10,000 in financial assets for their retirement.[1] 30 percent of households have no wealth or assets beyond their primary home.[2] And baby boomers, who are retiring by the thousands every day, 33 percent of them have less than $25,000.[3] It *is* scary out there. The fear of not having enough is a real fear for most. My hope for them is that they do not let the fear control them, that they can find a way to gather abundance to themselves.

I am assuming if someone has picked up a book like this on consciously managing money, they probably have some. For the fortunate few who do retire with a nest egg, the dreams they have were often designed when working under enormous pressure. Living those years under such stress encourages a lifestyle that seems necessary, at least until the stress dissipates, and the fear of not having "enough" can morph into comfort in the moment.

I believe all human beings just want to feel alive. Let me give you an example from my life. I have a deep-rooted desire to really be in the moment and enjoy it. When work does not provide me with this feeling—or, worse, diminishes my feeling of being

---

1    Sean Dennison, "64% of Americans Aren't Prepared For Retirement—and 48% Don't Care," GOBankingRates, September 23, 2019, https://www.gobankingrates.com/retirement/planning /why-americans-will-retire-broke/.

2    Financial Samurai, March 13, 2021, https://www.financialsamurai.com /percentage-wealth-outside-primary-residence/.

3    "1 In 3 Americans Have Less Than $5,000 In Retirement Savings," Northwestern Mutual, May 8, 2018, https://news.northwesternmutual .com/2018-05-08-1-In-3-Americans-Have-Less-Than-5-000-In -Retirement-Savings.

alive—I look elsewhere. I end up trying to create excitement or novelty, often by going out to eat at an expensive restaurant, shopping online, collecting vintage sneakers, or drinking a single malt scotch. Does this work? Rarely. Most of these "escapes" keep me trapped inside. Nine times out of ten, I would go to a restaurant and it would be a letdown. Sitting around for two hours does not make me feel alive. But cooking in my own beautiful kitchen? I've realized that *does* fill me with satisfaction. Frankly, those other escapes are mostly a waste of money, considering I work hard to pay the mortgage and property taxes on an amazing home directly across the street from Atlanta's premiere park. I had to remind myself to step away from society, that ten times out of ten, running on the grass, climbing a tree, or reading in the park makes my soul hum quietly.

# I DON'T KNOW YOUR NUMBER

The trappings of consumption, compounded by the social media—encouraged arms race that has us stockpiling selfies with palm trees in the background and custom Tom Ford shoes, really creates a lot of pressure. It's easy to lose track of what I find fulfilling when I let myself fall into a materialistic competition with others. It can easily distance me from myself and my goal of financial security. So, how much money do I need in retirement? I will never know until I am able to enjoy—I mean truly savor—life even while working. *My* life. Not based on the experiences or cool stuff that makes other people happy.

Case in point: so many people think retiring and then sailing around the world is what will make them happy. As proof this is hardly the case, there is a marina in the British Virgin Islands where you can get a whopping deal on a sailing yacht simply because it is the first stop out of Florida for many folks. That's right, the land lubbers buy a boat in Florida, stock the boat with many months of provisions, and then sail off into their dream sunset—only to learn before they make it to the first island that perhaps the sailing life is not really for them. They spent years fantasizing at their desks about some magical moment in the future, and sadly, so profoundly sadly, they harshly discovered that that day did not exist.

Another complicating factor in answering the question of "how much is enough?" has to do with the way we define wealth. It is not as easy to calculate as it once was. An outdated myth in society is that we need enough money piled up so we can live off the interest and never have to touch the principal. Historically, a gentleman living off his estate was one of the original definitions of wealth. I'm talking about the days of *Downton Abbey*, when an estate guaranteed longevity (that is, until season three). We do not need to mourn the passing of this age. It is an outdated definition that creates fear, scarcity, and anxiety. There is no rule that states you need to die at ninety with the same amount of money you had at sixty. Not only are you "allowed" to dip into your principal when you stop working, that is why you have it to begin with. What on earth are you going to do with all that money at age ninety anyway?

The hardest part of answering the question about

how much is enough is that I manage and advise on investments. But I am not a fortune teller. I don't know how long somebody is going to live, and I would need to know that to answer "how much do I need?" So, though understandable, it is an absurd question. The financial planning industry is predicated upon the fear that you won't have enough. The fear of being poor is so widespread, we have expressions such as "I don't want to be a bag lady" or, even worse, "I don't want to be eating cat food in my eighties."

My clients will often call me when they are considering a large purchase just to make sure they can afford it and still meet their goals. Most of the time, I encourage them to spend if they can connect the purchase to living life more fully. I suggest the same for you.

I'll never forget my client who called me a few years back. Full disclosure: this guy spent like a drunken sailor. I strongly encouraged him to save more and avoid large purchases, only for him to die a year and a half later with a sudden diagnosis of Lymphoma. This client enjoyed every moment of every day and every person he ran into. Because his money was slipping away, I felt like I needed to be a ballast for his optimism, but I wonder if he just knew—like deep-in-his-bones knew—he wouldn't make it to those golden years. What I know now is that he dispensed his money as freely as his love and that gave him joy. He was a beautiful example of living with abundance.

# HOARDING WON'T HELP

The two extreme stories that complicate our relationship with money and the answer to the question "how much is enough?" are this: "I may live until I am one hundred years old" or "I may die tomorrow." Is it any wonder that thought of money causes fear, frustration, indecisiveness, or complete avoidance?

You may live a long time and few will pay you for being old. Ideally, humans are rewarded by society for the value we provide via our words, thoughts, and actions—i.e., our human capital. In tribal societies a long, long time ago, elders who could no longer do physical labor were provided for because of the wisdom they provided. That is no longer the case in Western society today. With modern medicine, if you retire at sixty, you could legitimately live to a hundred.

That means you may be retired for more years than you actually spent in the workforce. But during those four decades, it is unlikely you will be given food, shelter, and care in return for your wisdom. Your human capital in today's Western society is only compensated when you are in the workforce. You need to store up financial capital when you have a chance, because the internet, Silicon Valley based apps, and twenty-year-old influencers are providing today's "wisdom." Your children may not be able to help you; as a matter of fact, you may still be asked to help support struggling children and grandchildren.

Therefore, it is almost natural and, in many ways, rational, for us to hoard money. If we are fortunate enough to make it to retirement age, it would be nice *not* to depend on others for our sustenance. *I better have enough*, you may tell yourself. *And since I don't know how much is enough, I better stockpile. It is better to be safe than sorry.*

This can spiral out of control. If I see the deployment of my money as a loss of my future security because I believe there is not enough, then will I hoard or overwork? At my worst, I will be stingy, greedy, and fearful. Well, what the heck is the point of having money if you are like that? Worse, still, if I connect my investment portfolio with my survival, I may spend the day watching the oftentimes ridiculous play-by-play of market entertainment on cable news and miss out on the fulfillment money can potentially provide to me and those around me.

Another belief that drives people to hoard is the Imposter Myth—it is common for a successful person to think of themselves as an imposter, or a charlatan, feeling they weren't as good as others thought and so didn't deserve the money they earned and there will be no way that they will ever earn it again. This is, of course, nonsense. It is hinged on another myth that is equally untrue: that a person earned whatever they have today on their own. Of course, that is not true. Many people and an entire societal system were in place in order for that person to be successful. So, if they didn't earn it all on their own, it is increasingly difficult to lose it all on their own. Don't get me wrong, the easiest way to make five million dollars is still to start with ten million. But no matter where you stand financially, a loss doesn't happen without warning signs.

# CULTIVATING A CONSCIOUS WEALTH MINDSET

So, how much *is* enough? How do I prepare for to-morrow and live today? How do I store enough for the future but not hoard? How do I balance abundance and scarcity? I know I can't time the market. I can't time my lifespan. So how much is enough? How do I prepare?

The first way to approximate the answers is a financial plan. The planning software that we have available today is quite sophisticated. You can create a plan that considers just about everything, including if you live to 105 and your cat gets gallstones. It factors in dozens of expenses with varying levels of inflation. You can assume the next great recession occurs during your first ten years of retirement or at some random date. It can assume you need long-term care starting at any given age and last for a determined amount of time. I encourage you to engage your advisor and get that number. It may scare you. On the other hand, it may make you feel at ease. Whatever the outcome, know that as soon as you put this plan to paper, it is dated. They call it a financial plan—not a financial reality. Almost as soon as you create your plan, reality changes. You need to stay up on it and revise it at least annually.

Yes, your plan is a backstop. The more effective backstop is cultivating a Conscious Wealth mindset.

This includes the conviction that we are enough—as mentioned in chapter 1—and the importance of distinguishing enhancements and enrichments, as outlined in chapter 2. Equally important is the *conviction that you have enough.*

# THE ENOUGH EQUATION

I made a formula to help with this. I call it my Enough Equation. "Enough" is my current financial assets and their growth, minus what I spend and will spend, plus my confidence to face adversity in the future, divided by my Money Memory. Here's how it works.

**E = My Current Financial Assets and Their Growth**

**− How Much I Spend and Will Spend**

**+ My Confidence to Face Adversity in the Future**

**/ Money Memory**

**ENOUGH**

Let's break that down:

$$E = \$ - S + C / MM$$

Enough =

- **My Current Financial Assets and Their Growth** = your stocks, bonds, businesses, land, intellectual property, etc., usually located on a Financial Net Worth Statement.

- **How Much I Spend and Will Spend** = your discretionary and nondiscretionary spending today, until that day you no longer need money (usually death, unless you are in the Hall and Oats song). Don't forget to account for inflation.
- **My Confidence to Face Adversity in the Future** = I have confidence that if my money goes away, I will rebuild.
- **Money Memory** = the sum total of your Money Memories and how it impacts your beliefs today. See chapter 1.

Below, I solve this equation for myself and model how you can solve on your own. A bit of warning: you are not going to end up with a number when you finish. You get that number in a financial plan. The point of this equation *is that money is relative and so is your Enough*. Don't worry, the work won't be in vain. It is an important exercise. Here we go . . .

## My Current Investment Assets

Personally, I have a financial net worth balance sheet that illustrates my financial assets, including an investment portfolio and a few rental properties. I also have equity in my advisory business. I boiled this part of the formula down to a number by doing a financial plan and I know what that money can provide under various conditions. I also have a fairly good idea of what that sum will look like in ten and then twenty years of growth. I feel confident that if things continue as they do, I'll be just fine and can stop working at a traditional retirement age, though I doubt I will. I really do enjoy my work.

*Minus*

## How Much I Spend

Far and away, the most important number to get down pat is how much we spend. But I hate budgets. I see them as constraints and they take so much time to keep updated. For me, I just look at two things to figure out my spending: my checking account and credit card bill. My checking account has information about my fixed expenses, like mortgage, utilities, and cars, so I know how much I need each month. Then I can determine and even categorize my discretionary spending by reading my credit card bill statements.

When I look at my spending over a given month, or year, I see that I spend a lot on food, as well as hobbies like sailing. These are the two most important *things* to me that I try to keep as flexible expenses. Although I own a one-person racing sailboat, I charter the big ones to go on trips. Sure, it may cost more to rent, but I can drop the contract anytime. Before, I used to think affluent people owned boats. That's nonsense, of course. There is an old expression: rich enough to rent. It's the idea that you have enough money to spend on one-time experiences, like a cabin on a lake for the month and then walk away from it. Most people think renting is throwing money away but, really, it is holding on to your autonomy. Under a renting scenario, I can scale back if needed.

*Plus*

## My Confidence to Face Adversity in the Future

This one is not so easily quantifiable but vital information to know about yourself. I know that disasters can hit at any time. I take some solace in the fact that when the biggest disasters hit, they will erase all my fears about money. If I ever get a call at two in the morning with terrible news, or hear a doctor's diagnosis and feel a heat radiate through my entire body, I know I will realize that money is not, in reality, the biggest issue. Sure, I occasionally have a fear arise that I may lose my financial assets one day, but I'm actually okay with that. Sometimes I am secretly (or not so secretly anymore, since you're reading this) interested to see what I would do. In my heart, I know I would be okay and may find a lot of enjoyment in starting over. If I had to give myself a rank on a scale of 1 to 10 on my ability to face future adversity, 10 being fully ready to face challenges, I guess I would give myself a 9.

*Divided by*

## Money Memory Awareness

If you can figure out roughly how much you spend and then divide that by your current impression or feelings about the state of your financial situation, you can decide if you have "enough." Money Memories carry a lot of weight. For me, it's that I grew up in a modest household with shared bedrooms, and everything was a hand-me-down; I rode my

Aunt Shellie's bike with a wire basket until the age of twelve. I never had much of an expectation to be rich, because, honestly, I didn't even know what "rich" was as a kid. You'll recall, I still don't have a particularly high desire for material goods. Thus, my Money Memory sets a pretty low bar and allows me to live a life of abundance because I don't expect much. The good news is that my experiences with scarcity as a child—eating Tums, raisin-less Raisin Bran, and drinking Jell-O—were not all for naught.

### Answer

Processing my financial life through the Enough Equation, I know I have enough. I just feel it in my bones. I have enough now. I believe in myself. I will find money in the future if everything goes away—I have more than my past-self ever thought he'd have. And I can scale back my expenses pretty quickly if needed.

> **If you do the equation and reach the same conclusion, I recommend you go open a window and scream, "Hell yeah! I don't need to worry about money!"**

I get it . . . just typing this sounds weird, a bit braggy, and in poor taste. It's not like I go around telling everybody I meet "I have enough!" I'm not ashamed of it, it's just they would not understand. What I am really saying is that I spend and will spend less than I have or will have and, if it all goes to hell, I have the confidence and the Money Memory to support my new reality. And if that is true, I have enough!!!

This is great news, because I have bigger fish to fry than money. I want to be part of something special and meaningful. I want my life to count for something. Nobody else can define this for me—nor can they take it away. Cars, boats, houses, they can disappear overnight. Even if they don't disappear overnight, they could slowly lose their flavor until they become meaningless possessions.

My Enough Equation's bottom line is really about abundance and fulfillment.

Scarcity of money is only a reality when I don't believe in myself. But I *do* believe in myself, and I know I don't need material things to be happy. I enjoy them and find ways to have and things I want, but I don't let them put too much pressure on the rest of my equation. I believe that whatever comes my way, I will always be able to make enough money to thrive. Even if my financial plan does not work out and for some reason I am working until I'm seventy-five, I believe that is for a good reason. I will probably find joy and meaning in that work and will be happy that I can still contribute.

Abundance is my reality. I don't need to hoard. I don't need to be stressed. I don't need to see other people's success as a threat to mine. I have a Conscious Wealth mindset, which means not only do I have enough, I am enough.

# YOUR STORY

Now, let's return to writing your money story. Here are some questions for consideration:

- When you think back, was your childhood one of abundance or one of scarcity? How does that shape you now?
- Do you have a number in your head that you need to accumulate before you feel safe? What is that number based on?
- How do you define what it means to be "wealthy"? Is it attainable?
- Have you ever hit your number only to push out a new, higher number?
- If you died today, what would be your single biggest regret?
- Are you going to die tomorrow or live forever?
- Are you stockpiling money? How much is enough?
- Solve for E =

# LEVEL TWO

# PURPOSE

# CHAPTER 4
# HOW DID I GET HERE?

**Let's level up.** It's time to move from "I have enough" to "I am enough!" From Abundance to Purpose. Time to focus your efforts on being the person you were born to be, and to spend time and money on things that bring out that person. Which is good, because some of that "person" has been bruised and buried during your quest for financial wealth.

**Once past the fear of scarcity, you will be able to heal your relationship with your work, family, and business—much of what may have been neglected or misdirected in your quest for financial wealth.**

## USING PASSION TO FIND PURPOSE

In chapter 2, we touched on how passion can lead us to finding something that gives purpose to our lives. American Trappist Monk Thomas Merton stated, "The tree gives glory to God by being a tree." In the end, we can best find purpose in this world when we can just stop *doing* for a moment and just be.

When I tried to redirect my passion for photographing scenes of "real life" into something less meaningful (taking staged portraits in order to pay the bills), the camera suddenly felt heavy, like a burden. Going to work did not provide me energy. I was no longer connecting with others on a deeper level, which had made me feel real and whole. I was not giving glory to God, as Thomas Merton said.

As a matter of fact, not being true to my passion actually killed it—I no longer use my camera. Oh, don't worry, I have multiple passions, all of which provide me with a sense of purpose. I love to cook and serve others in the kitchen; it is my love language. I write, or sometimes I produce podcasts; both are an enjoyable creative outlet, and I like knowing my words may inspire like minds. I also formally study psychotherapy and counseling and use it to learn who I am in relation to others.

My biggest passion, teaching, has led me to my job as a financial advisor where I am connected and know I am doing something important, cultivating confidence and happiness in my clients—and giving them the opportunity to give back to the world by consciously employing their wealth. I go to work each day energized and bring my real self. Every day I go to work and I build upon my talents and strengths, I am stripping away a layer that covers up my purpose. I've created and work with a team of professionals who I encourage and empower to do the same.

# TESTING YOUR RESOLVE

On your journey to wealth creation, you can't just mentally picture "abundance" and wait for it to fall in your lap. Chances are, you had a vision and *then made it happen*. Along the way, you were surprised multiple times and almost surely felt like quitting more than once. You bobbed, weaved, pivoted (as it is so trendy to say now) until you found a viable business plan that the world wanted and was willing to pay for. You likely didn't just create a plan and then stuck to it, no matter what. There are two approaches to the adventure, two approaches that differ in their manner of dealing with obstacles—are you a mountaineer or a sailor?

I'm not the mountain climbing type. I think you either are or you are not. I've asked mountain climbing types what is up there, on the top of that mountain, and they often jab their chest with two thumbs inward, saying, "This guy!"

It's not like that kind of pride isn't earned; it's no small feat to scale a mountain. That choice entails months of training your legs, lungs, and mind, and honing your sheer determination to achieve the final goal. It also takes planning, proper equipment, and even good fortune. If you are not a Sherpa, it may cost a fortune. Many climbers use visualization practices to see themselves climbing the hill before it occurs. Once they get started, it's game-on, though. They single-mindedly climb Mount You-Name-It. One step is followed with another, and another, until the goal is reached. Part of the mental exercise of climbing a mountain is you do not allow for any alternatives other than to reach the top. If there is a voice on day four of the climb that whispers *This is stupid, why am I doing this?* it is quickly shushed. One of the tactics these climbers use to get to the top is to rarely stop for long, because that might give them time to reflect on why they are climbing the mountain. The flip side of that coin, however, is that they are not slowing down to contemplate less risky methods or courses when the path becomes obscured. They just keep taking step after step. The reason, and then the intent, to climb that mountain was cemented in their mind before they set off.

I am the sailing type. My dream is to sail into blue waters to beautiful locations and lose sight of land (which, I know from experience, I really do enjoy). There is some physical fitness needed to sail a big ship in big seas, but let's face it, Captain Hook wasn't the only sailor to do it with a peg leg or a hook as a hand. The preparation for sailing is about having the right provisions (food and water) and a sail-worthy ship. There's also a fair amount of knowledge of water and boats and knots required. The biggest difference between the mountain climber and the sailor is that the sailor has all the time in the world to reflect. In fair weather, the boat sails itself and the captain is given hours upon hours to stare out at the blue ocean and skies. With little sleep, little to distract, and ample time, the tiny voice that says, *Why in the world am I doing this*? cannot be shushed.

It is quite common to be in the middle of a long voyage, stuck in quiet solitude, and question why you left the dock in the first place. At first it was the excitement and hope for adventure getting the sailor up in the morning, but after awhile, the boredom and danger leaves that reason behind. You may find yourself taking on just enough water to keep you working your tail off, but not enough to sink. And not just figuratively. The first solo, nonstop circumnavigation Gold Globe race in 1968 was composed of nine men who started in England, setting off to sail the world alone, without stopping, and each of them came to a point they intensely questioned their resolve. Given time to think, they quavered. All but two ended the journey prematurely, some in shipwreck or death. Only one man finished, and, so, by default won. The other survivor made it three quarters of the way and decided he didn't care about winning, so sailed to the tropical island of Tahiti instead.

When faced with the strength of *your* resolve, you can climb a mountain, moving forward with no time for reflection that would test your resolve, or you can sail across the seas, reflection a major element of the trip. What type of adventurer are you?

I bring up these two contrasting styles of adventure as an analogy for wealth creation. If you have worked for and brought about personal financial wealth—whatever the dollar amount—you have been on a serious journey that almost certainly tested your resolve. It is likely you have had doubts along the way and have had to redefine your motivation mid course. Perhaps you made it to the top and wondered if the course you'd settled on was the right one. In the following chapters, I share my journey to worldly "success" and highlight ways that destruction became part of my story, and how my resolve to find holistic abundance kept me going. But for now, back to being resolute with your purpose . . .

# A LESSON ON COURSE CORRECTIONS

In 2008, I was living in Brazil, no longer teaching but still exploring all the avenues in photography, trying to make it work. As I mentioned, I had drifted from my spiritually themed photography, shooting photos of spontaneous religious manifestations and spiritual pilgrimages, to photographing brides, pregnant women, and models for a fee. I was unhappy, working for money but without purpose.

Around that time, I took a quick trip back to the states. Once home, I found out my parents had been shielding a truth from me, that my father's health was terrible and their business was up for sale. Hatton's Deli, the restaurant he had spent his entire life running, was literally killing him—he'd been on his feet day in and day out for decades and now his hips were partially fused at the joint. He was in dire need of hip replacement surgery . . . five years before. However, selling a shuttered restaurant wasn't going to solve his financial needs; a restaurant is not a restaurant if there aren't customers coming through the doors. Selling a closed business is really just selling a building.

I reluctantly stepped in. Someone had to keep Hatton's Deli alive, so my dad could sell the business and all its clients, not just square footage.

In the span of a few weeks, I went from shooting models in the south of Brazil to flipping hamburgers and frying over four hundred wings a day in Cleveland, Ohio. Talk about cultural whiplash. I settled back into my hometown, determined to get this restaurant sold.

My father and I worked every day. He had me go to the farmer's market, organize schedules, hire, fire, you name it. Essentially, I was a proxy manager. I would fill in for an employee who'd been "overserved" the night before or just didn't feel like coming in. One day I worked the short-order grill and the next day I was making catering deliveries.

It took us about five months and a lot of setbacks, but we finally sold the business. My dad paid his debts and was able to go home, get the surgery, and rest.

I will never forget the last night at the restaurant. I was locking the back door and, in joking, ceremonious fashion, cocked my head to the side and said to my father, "Any final words you'd like to share?" My quip sounded like a narrator in a documentary.

My dad looked at me, let out a sigh, and mumbled a curse word. Then he slowly turned around, aided by his walker, and started the ten-minute hobble to his car parked twenty yards away.

When I got in the car, I asked in a caring-yet-exasperated tone, "Dad, what the heck happened? How did it come to this?" Meaning, how did it come to pass that all of his equity was wrapped up in the business, and he was physically broken and aged beyond his sixty-something years?

His answer was clear and self-aware. I will paraphrase: "The safe thing to do was to keep the restaurant in the city. Stay put, maintain the restaurant location even though all my customers were moving out into the suburbs. Sure, the restaurant started as a Jewish-style deli, but as the demographics in the neighborhood changed, I would add wings, macaroni and cheese, meatloaf . . . but before you knew it, nobody knew what we did anymore."

We once had the best corned beef in town, as the large neon sign out front bragged for decades. (At the time of sale, only some of the neon worked and had flakes of white paint chips missing). My father generously nourished the city, provided employment for hundreds, and created real value for others, but nobody really knew what Hatton's stood for anymore.

If we are categorizing my dad, he is the mountain climber, moving too fast, too resolutely, and admittedly with too much fear to question the climb. Instead of making the bold move to change course, he adapted to the ever-changing neighborhood. He felt he should have taken the risk, shed his father's restaurant and expectations, and started something new and risky. In hindsight, that would have been the restaurant's best chance for success.

**Now, when the journey was called off because of age and health, he had real regrets. His wealth creation was accompanied by destruction and in many ways, it was too late to rebuild.**

My father's words and situation stuck with me as I returned to Brazil, to the fledgling photography business I was starting to despise and that had surprisingly not failed in my extended absence. However, I was far from busy or flush with spending cash. I started looking at my life choices rather soberly.

Here I was, thirty-three years old, a world traveler who had cultivated a wide range of skills ... I was booked with paying photography gigs, but I had no career, I wasn't seen as an expert. I was about the age my father was when he needed to have taken a big risk to right the ship. I did not know what I wanted, but I felt like I needed a career. Teaching was a career, but it killed me, seeing all my students move on while I stayed put, forced into stagnation by administration. Like my students, I wanted to learn new things. I wanted to have a trade, a skill, or a career where nobody could hold me back or take anything away from me, and I wanted to be respected for my expertise. My goal was set. I had determined the mountain I was going to climb: Mount Get-a-Career.

# CLIMBING THE MOUNTAIN

I decided to call my uncle, a financial advisor. He took an hour out of his busy day to answer my questions and give me the confidence I needed. He told me I had what it took to be successful in his industry and he helped me see I had the theoretical knowledge through my studies of economics, as well as the practical knowledge after owning my small photography business. He'd started his career in the industry when he was about my age, coming off both a divorce and a business bankruptcy. It had been a one-eighty for him, too. And although he would never say it, he'd become one of the best advisors in Ohio—one who really understood the markets, built portfolios, and actually managed money. He never saw himself as a salesman of company products but, rather, he saw himself as a student of the markets who served his clients.

I got off the phone and headed to Sao Paulo's main thoroughfare. Avenida Paulista was my place to go to hang out among the crowds, an area loaded with banks, marketing agencies, museums, and cafés. I slipped into the Starbucks, as I often did, took out a book, and began to read. This time it was Herman Hesse's *Siddhartha*, a book about Buddha. The following passage caught my attention:

> *Siddhartha walked through the forest, was already far from the city, and knew nothing but that one thing, that there was no going back for him, that this life, as he had lived it for many years until now, was over and done away with, and that he had tasted all of it, sucked everything out of it until he was disgusted with it.*

I reread the line again and again. Here I sat, doing the elitist thing, drinking a black coffee at Starbucks . . . drinking an American coffee in Brazil, the land of world-renowned coffee. As I looked around the exquisite shopping district, I knew it was time to go home. I realized how, in my personal exile, I'd immersed myself in foreign cultures and never looked back, but I'd just now chosen to be American.

I'd had a good run living overseas, traveling for twelve years and visiting over forty countries, but the excitement of wandering and exploring had dwindled.

I needed a stronger sense of purpose. It's why I'd felt so much discomfort returning to Brazil, where I had no direction, especially after closing up my father's deli. This pivotal moment was a chance to pause mid voyage. My uncle had suggested a career in finance. Could he be right?

I got up and walked down the bustling street in a dreamlike state, knowing it would be one of my last days there. I remember getting to my apartment and calling my mother, telling her I was returning home. I said I was finally starting a career and would need to crash at their home in Cleveland until I found a job. I excitedly told her my new plan, that I'd decided to go into financial services. I enjoyed the theory of economics, the practice of owning a business, and the daily interaction with others

"But, Brandon, you don't really like people," Mom replied, confused.

*Thud.* Oh, the pleasures of telling your wildest dreams to people that you love. She was not trying to be mean or discouraging, she was just trying to figure it out in the moment. To her credit, most people don't understand introverts. I could have been really hurt or disheartened, but instead, after a beat, I laughed and said we would figure that part out later. I was full speed ahead to the top of Mount Get-a-Career.

I took the Herman Hesse book to heart, selling and giving away most of my possessions, returning home with two medium-sized boxes and a carry-on. Returning to live with my parents as a man in my early thirties presented its own set of challenges, but it was nice to have a place where I could begin to rebuild.

The late 2008 economy was not aware of my plans to start a career in the financial industry. I had a few phone interviews with a company in Atlanta and flew into town for a day to interview for a position I really wanted. The conversations were fruitful, but the industry was in the middle of a hiring freeze. The universe was not providing in the way I expected.

After not finding a job for several months, especially not with the one I wanted in Atlanta, I took a last-minute trip to Cozumel to go diving. It was the first week of December, and I knew I now wouldn't likely be hired until the New Year. It was only when the tires of the plane lifted off the ground that the obvious hit me: if I wanted to get a job in Atlanta, then I had to move there, job or no job.

I came home in a buzz and spent the holidays with my parents, and then, on New Year's Day, 2009, I once again loaded up my belongings, this time into the trunk of my mother's old Chrysler Sebring convertible (complete with a rosary bumper sticker), which she'd given to me for Christmas. After handing her back the Yanni, Rod Stewart, and Michael Bublé CDs from the glove compartment and giving her a kiss, I drove down to Atlanta.

I had made this type of voyage many times before. It was the type of voyage my grandparents embarked on a century ago and that immigrants do daily. It is the same voyage I embarked on when I went to Egypt, Lebanon, and Brazil. I knew I could survive anywhere.

I entered the city with a sense of freedom, few possessions, and a mission. I was on fire. I knew I was taking a big risk, but I didn't plan on just surviving, I was going to thrive. Filled with optimism and excitement, and luckily for me, with enough savings from years of traveling lightly overseas, I drove the streets of my new home town.

On day one in Atlanta, I settled into my room in a shared house I'd found on Craigslist and went to the mall to buy a suit. At that time, I only had one suit for interviews. I figured it would be nice to pick up a second, but then I heard about this well-known store that seemed to have these amazing sales where if you bought one suit, you could get two for free. I mean, that sounded like a deal too good to pass up, so I naively rushed to the store. Of course, later I heard this sale pretty much runs all year round, but that is how green I was in this world.

At this "super sale of the century," I ran into the guy who'd interviewed me for the job I wanted.

He was surprised to see me. "What are you doing in town? And why aren't you working with us yet?"

"Your company hasn't offered me a job yet!" We laughed, and I told him they were my first choice. I got a call from the company the next day, letting me know I was on the top of their hiring list. We remained in contact for the next six months, waiting for the hiring freeze to end.

In the meantime, I was looking for any work I could find. I eventually took a job as a personal banker at a regional bank, which is one step above a bank teller. My job was to greet customers and cross-sell as much as possible. "Would you like a car loan with that check deposit? Why are you taking out so much money on your credit card? Perhaps a home equity line of credit is more suitable." I was to "sling" as much company product to as many people as I possibly could. The stress and pressure on bank tellers, personal bankers, and bank managers was enormous, though never really got to me. I was not there long enough, nor did I take it that seriously. This job was just a stepping stone for me. What *was* getting to me was the lack of movement on my goals.

I remember sitting at the steps of the art museum in Atlanta, talking out loud to myself, wondering if I was close to a breakdown. I needed something to happen. I had taken so many risks and needed something to give. *I did not move from the south of Brazil to be a personal banker. I came here to be an expert in my field!*

With this uncertainty about my future came discomfort. Part of me wanted to do everything within my power to make this discomfort go away: go back to teaching, move to another country, try something new. But another part of me felt I needed to be more comfortable with the uncertainty, to just ride out my unhappiness with this job. What I didn't know at the time was that this was my moment to reconsider my current headlong climb to the top of Mount Get-a-Career. The universe was providing me with a way out of what could become a years-long slog of fighting a system that was not aligned to my values. Yet, despite the lessons I'd learned from my father's heartbreak, I denied myself the gift of listening and reflecting. I decided to keep climbing.

The very next day I was given the opportunity I'd been aiming for, the job that was to quickly propel me further up the mountain: I got the call that the hiring freeze had thawed where I wanted to be hired, and I was welcome to join in three weeks. I smiled, quit my banking job, and flew to Mexico for one last vacation before the work began. I knew it was going to be hard but I had no idea just how hard it would be.

To become a financial advisor, I had to study and take the Series 7—passing the exam would allow me to sell registered investments. I absolutely loved studying the enormous amount of material for this exam. It was fun for me. Many advisors hated taking the exam. I don't blame them; if you are under contract with a firm and don't pass, you're fired on the spot.

## NOT STOPPING TO REFLECT

Training began on day one at the firm. I arrived and they pointed me to my chair at a large desk, which accommodated twelve people. No cubicles, no half walls. Taped to my computer screen were sign-on instructions. I sat down and began the online courses.

The training program takes two years at the large firms, but you are expected to start creating revenue for the firms as soon as you pass the exams, which needs to happen within ninety day of hiring. If the test doesn't get you, the sales goals may send you packing. The sales goals are very high; 90 percent of advisors are fired before the end of year one.

We also had weekly group training in our complex. Those meetings were excruciating. I was a teacher, trained in pedagogy, and had high expectations on what training should look like. I also had huge sales hurdles I needed to hit in order to stay at the firm. Yet,

I was stuck in an oversized conference room role-playing sales calls on a weekly basis for two years. We also had "experts" come in and tell us how to make eye contact, how to choose power clothing options, how to do a firm handshake (I kid you not!), and how to pitch the firm's latest products. Ideally, they could have taught us economics, finance, history of markets, portfolio construction—you name it—anything but how to smile and dial a phone.

If you haven't guessed it by now, I was kicked out of the training program's meetings. I was a bit too vocal in my criticisms of the pedagogy (if you can call it that) and the "sparkling" products we were expected to sell. My real training came from reading research on Saturday and Sunday mornings with a mug of coffee while nestled in my comfy chair. I also took specific courses for financial advisors, such as the Chartered Retirement Planning Counselor and the Chartered Advisor in Philanthropy. I read countless books on investing and the economy and weekly financial research reports. I have never obsessed over the market on a daily basis. To this day, there are times I don't see what the market is doing because I am too busy looking at more important things.

I was one of the lucky ones. I entered the program after knowing how to learn on my own. I studied and had woven economics into all my history classes. I had an uncle I could call at any time and ask for honest feedback about the latest product they put in front of me. It was nerve-wracking at times and it created a lot of discomfort.

**I was given warning signs that perhaps I was not on the right course, but I didn't want to stop and think about it . . . I had a mountain to climb.**

And climb I did. I built a loyal client base by earning their trust and giving them a voice in their financial decisions. Everything was going well until my shitty Volvo moment.

# THE GREAT VOLVO AWAKENING

I opened the door to my Volvo and slid onto the black fabric seat in a way that would not tear my expensive pinstripe suit on the worn seat bolster. With the flick of my wrist, I turned the key and music blared. I hastily jabbed at the volume, silencing the evidence of my optimism earlier that day. The car was sickly hot. Heat emanated from the seats and my stomach burned. It was the kind of heat that starts in your stomach, rises to your chest, and makes you lightheaded.

It was spring. Or summer. There really was not a big difference in Georgia. Dumb car to have in Georgia, but I thought it looked cool.

I opened the window but that didn't help. I put the air conditioning on high, but hot air from the vents smacked me in the face. I felt beads of sweat forming across my scalp. I opened my mouth to allow for more oxygen. It was not getting better. *How long does it really take to get cold air in this thing?* Somebody later told me that Volvo was a luxury-ish car, not really a luxury car. They were right. The day I'd bought it, I felt like the luckiest guy in the world, but in that moment, it might as well have been a Toyota CR2 with a spoiler, rims, and a decal.

This car was not special. Neither was I.

It was the lowest point in my professional career, and indeed my adult life, but not because of the stupid car. I had just left the dentist office in my stupid pinstripe suit, climbing into what I believed to be a fancy black-on-black turbo-charged Volvo.

Moments before, the oral surgeon told me I needed to have a biopsy.

I remember thinking, *Hey, Doc, don't worry about me. I am solid as a rock. Nothing will shake me. I got this. I am fine.* And it was true. I was calm as the receptionist made the appointment for the biopsy, at least until the point she casually said, "Oh, and make sure you bring a friend or family member. They will need to be in the room the entire time and take you home."

It didn't hit me until I sat down in that hot-as-hell Volvo. I had no one. My family was in another state. My girlfriend had just dumped me because I was always working, and when I was around, I was "never present." I had no real work friends, not anyone who would want to lose a half day to take me to the hospital. And I definitely did not want to be perceived as a weak person who needed help.

Yep, it was official, I had climbed the wrong mountain. I had missed the turn-off way too many times.

I had been lying to myself for years. I'd clung to something to make myself feel good. The work was grueling. The hours obscene. The other employees were not people I wanted as friends. The pace erased any fulfillment. In these early years, I was helping normal people who had just reached retirement age and yet, because of the terrible economy, barely had enough money to scrape by. Or I was talking to people getting laid off in their midfifties and not having enough to show for it. Now, they planned to work until they were in their seventies. They had not planned for the great recession. Nor did they didn't take into account the rampant ageism in American corporations.

I loved these clients and took amazing care of them, but I also pitied them. I swore to myself that no way would that be me. I would not be eaten up by the system and spit out. I would build something great for myself.

I would build a fortress around myself so I would not be vulnerable to the fluctuations of the market. I would save everything and create a fortune. I was clever, I told myself. I was sacrificing my time and happiness now because one day I would make all this money and it would be worth it. One day, I would have an office with a door. One day, I could choose my clients . . .

Wait.

## I was already here. The day had arrived and it was all a lie.

I'd already made it. I had the office, the admin, the salary, the prestige, and, yet, I was as powerless as ever. I was "rich" but alone.

During the first stage of my financial career, I prided myself on the fact that I did no harm. I did good work and lived up to a high code of ethics. But, having said that, my basic exchange with other human beings was, "If you give me money, I will give you more." And I think at the heart of the financial transaction, that is what money management is about to many advisors and clients. Everybody who works makes some kind of exchange. If you work for a large corporation, the exchange may sound like, "If you give me your time and energy, I'll give you money." The problem is, you only have so much time and energy to give. And in many cases, a company will never tell you to stop giving. Or they may tell you, but they hardly believe it. They may sing the praises of work/life balance, but if you are not careful, they will walk you to your grave with "attaboys" and pay raises as your marriage, family life, and health deteriorate. Just about everybody knows of somebody who has died of a heart attack at work. Man, what a sad way to go.

## ARE YOU A COMMODITY?

Ideally, a company should offer, "If you give us time and energy, we will provide you with money, dignity, and purpose." But because that was so far away from my beginning viewpoint, it would have seemed like a foreign language to me when I started. So I worked, and worked, and I ended up commoditizing myself.

I based my worth only on how much money I could make people.

This was the framework in which I placed my trade, thus clients valued me based on how much money I could make them. Funny how that happens—people treat you the way you instruct them to treat you. And when you become a one-trick pony with a binary result—you do or you don't jump over the whatever—you are commoditized. And commodities are hard to connect to. After all, why would you connect to a *thing*? That's about as silly as saying "please" to Siri. It is just there to serve a specific purpose. And when "it" no longer serves that means to an end, it can be disposed of.

The more inhuman I felt, the more I felt the need to grow my business and to do so quickly, even though this meant not being as close to my clients. Yet, despite the wall I'd built between me and them, I gave good advice. Nobody was complaining.

I believed I had to grow, because in time I would eventually get fired by clients who saw me as dispensable. I remember a senior advisor telling me that being an advisor was like piling stuff up in a truck. You had to keep piling on new clients because inevitably some will fall off. Even at the time, it was the dumbest analogy I ever heard. You can see the vicious cycle forming here: the company creates an environment that encourages you to commoditize yourself, you work harder, and if you fail, die, or leave, the client just plugs somebody else in your place. It shouldn't be that hard to replace you; after all, you are a commodity. Trapped.

Not only did I have this type of relationship with my clients, my company also saw me as a commodity. A commoditized person fits really well into large institutions and is replaceable. To be replaceable is not bad from an institution's viewpoint, because continuity is needed if a worker walks out the door. Much of the financial services industry is designed to commoditize its workers and keep the clients at the firm as long as possible. Clients are called "sticky," meaning the more cross-selling you do, the stickier they become. Not very humane or loving in my opinion.

But there is a major moral hazard when the worker who is supposed to be giving advice that will impact another human being's entire life is feeling less than human. I can't say whether my clients knew I was not there a hundred percent, but looking back at it, I was cheating myself out of fulfillment. I was uncomfortable once more.

Mercifully, the car finally cooled down. I sat there, wracking my brain for someone, anyone, who could pick me up from the hospital after this biopsy. Crazily enough, there was a real chance I could have cancer, but I didn't care. I was not worried about dying. I was most upset that I was living alone and that I had seemingly wasted years of my life trying to climb Mount Get-a-Career. The vista didn't seem worth it.

So, I did what any self-respecting momma's boy would do: I called my mom. I explained the doctor visit, not the car incident. My mom worked in radiation oncology and recommended I move forward with the biopsy. She had seen too many cases of people thinking *Oh, it's nothing*, only to learn too late that, *Ohh, it is indeed something*. She offered to fly down, but I assured her I would be okay. Here I was again, doing it alone.

I drove home. That is what I do, I plow forward. On the way, maneuvering through the midtown streets, my mind went through a labyrinth of possibilities only to realize each one hit a dead end. I could ask Angie at work—*No that won't work. She is under the same pressure as me*. I could ask my girlfriend—*Wait, I don't have one anymore*. I could ask my landlord—*Oh, that won't work*. And besides, who thinks that?

I eventually found a friend to take me to the hospital. He was the last guy I called because I thought he would be too wrapped up in his job to want to give me his time. Surprisingly, he jumped at the opportunity and put aside his work for the day to help me. I was glad to see him in the waiting room, in his typical manner, flirting with the women in white in the office. I was so loopy on the way home. We still laugh about the banter that ensued that day. He was a great sport and a true friend I did not know I had.

As the doctor predicted, the biopsy was thankfully negative, and I was back to work within a week. The only catch? I had stitches in my mouth and was unable to speak. I'd have to spend the next week in complete silence.

**I had plenty of time to think about my lack of wealth in every way except money.**

It was time to change course. To once again find a way to be the person I was born to be. I certainly wasn't born to be that guy slumped in my Volvo, unhappy, alone and disconnected from family and friends. I resolved to readjust how I spent my time and money, making sure I focused on building the me that I wanted to be, that I was meant to be.

# YOUR STORY

I know you must have experienced something like this in your life, or maybe you are experiencing it now, questioning the path you are on. Taking a moment to reflect on these questions should be helpful. I recommend writing out the answers as well as talking them through with a friend. Interrogating these ideas both verbally and in writing will generate answers from different parts of your brain.

- What is the biggest risk you've taken? Were you running from something or to something?
- Would you take that risk again?
- Which adventurer do you most connect with—the sailor or the mountaineer? What makes you think that?
- What risks seemed really big at the time and in hindsight seemed like the obvious choice?
- How do you feel about these statements?
- All things work out in the end. If it's not working out, it's not the end yet.
- The universe will provide.
- Can you sit with uncertainty? How quickly do you take action to avoid uncertainty?
- Considering Thomas Merton's quote, do you live with purpose now?

# CHAPTER 5
# WHAT DO YOU DO WHEN YOU GET TO THE WRONG TOP?

**Traumatic events are the perfect time to stop, look around, and reevaluate.** The famous fourteenth century Persian poet Hafiz spoke of this, loosely translated as: "The first thing a fish needs to say is 'Something ain't right about this camel ride—And I'm feeling so damn thirsty.'"[4]

Is it time for you to transition to something else? It was for me. I was tired of feeling empty.

## THE WRONG MOUNTAIN

Here I was, a mouth full of stitches, under doctor's orders to not speak for at least seven days. I worked in the financial services industry . . . not an easy task. Yet, while not talking was hard, being forced to just listen was eye opening and painful.

You'd think a good financial advisor would already be a good listener, but that was not the culture back

---

4    Excerpt of "Damn Thirsty," modified from the original, from the Penguin publication *The Gift: Poems by Hafiz*, by Daniel Ladinsky, copyright 1999 and used with permission.

in 2009. The advisors around me were more like what most people thought of when I told them I managed investments for families, and they pictured me in front of a computer screen, trading stocks all day, calling in pork belly orders on the phone with bursts of screaming, "Buy, buy, buy!" For me, this couldn't be further from the truth, even back then. I'd normally spend half of my time on the phone with my clients. But, to be fair, back then I did a lot of the talking. I was wired for sound.

Returning to work, I put the phone down and barely spoke a word for a week. I saw this as a form of silent meditation and embraced it. I knew I needed something to change. I had made it to the top of the mountain—as a successful mountain climber does—only to realize it was the wrong mountain.

I started to hear and see things that had been around me for years. And I did not like it. In this silence, I started to unravel how I got to where I was. Here I was at the top of the mountain, mute and powerless, wondering how the heck I even got to the apex. I looked around, went to work, and listened.

Nobody at the office knew about my appointment, much less that I was there with stitches in my mouth. A friend of mine asked me if my employers would make accommodations for my return. I snickered inwardly. What a nice thought. *Accommodations? What are accommodations?* I worked in a place where if you did not yell or become extremely aggressive, you did not get your needs met. The hyper-masculine culture required you to speak up and often.

For example, one time long before the stitches, a partner in the firm made a joke at my expense in front of my peers. I let it slide in the moment but followed him to his office to confront him.

"Look, it's fine if we joke amongst ourselves, but let's not do that in front of my peers," I told him. I hoped my honest, direct approach would suffice

He puffed out his chest. "Do you even know who you are talking to right now?" he asked, meaning that I was addressing a partner of the firm.

"Yes. A person who will have to pick himself up off the floor after I kick his ass the next time he does that," I responded. This type of aggressive dominance was uncharacteristic but I knew if I wavered, he would do it again, just to prove his authority.

Instead of yelling at me, he conceded. "I'm sorry."

I turned on my heel and left his office, shaking with adrenaline. I hated the person I had to be in order to be "successful" in this world.

But back to my silent meditation. There were no accommodations. I just sat in my office and did my work. I didn't reach out to anyone or ask for anything and they, in turn, hardly acknowledged I wasn't talking. They were too caught up in their own world.

## In my silence, I heard, felt, and saw greed.

As just one small example, we had a girl on the desk we called Annuity Anastasia. She was Russian and sold every one of her clients an annuity. She argued they needed the guaranteed fixed income. We all shook our head, knowing she was the one guaranteed an income selling those expensive products.

Excessive, dirty freaking greed.

And you know what they say: *if you spot it, you got it.* We all had it. It was ruining our lives and ruining the lives in our wake. I heard a senior partner chuckle when a junior partner bought a Rolex, saying, "Now we got him!" He knew this young pup would have to keep longer hours to live a lifestyle he was slowly slipping into.

The materialistic drive was obvious since my early days on the job, back when I was still working at that big twelve-person desk. I will never forget the guy next to me, on my first day, pulling out a stack of custom shirts from under his desk, each individually tied in a bow. He said, in a low drawn-out voice, "Duuuuude, I've got a shirt hook-up for you."

Apparently, my off-the-rack shirts were not good enough. As a teacher and an artist, I'd already been struggling with not feeling like I was good enough to be in the corporate culture. Apparently, my insecurity was based on a truth, at least in their eyes. I did not dress like them, flop my hair like them, or root for their collegiate football teams on the weekends.

Despite this, I knew I could outwork them. I figured my work would get me in, not my style. So, I did the right thing for my clients and kept my head down. I took some serious financial hits when I was starting out. I missed major bonus milestones because I did not sell my clients on what I considered expensive garbage that paid high commissions. I've never regretted doing the right thing, but it is hard to live surrounded by greed and not have some of it rub off on you.

When I say surrounded by greed, I mean literally. I worked in a building where the alphabet soup of banks were located: Morgan Stanly, Merrill Lynch, US Trust, UBS. Nobody said hello to one another in the lobbies. These people were the competition. We made more than 90 percent of the people in that city, and signs of obvious wealth were everywhere, yet every financier walking through that lobby looked lonely. And miserable.

Financial advisors are notorious for living beyond their means. Many of them spend so much money trying to look rich, with $2,000 suits, bull and bear cufflinks, Porsche 911s, and Rolex watches, that they end up in poor financial condition. It is a typical case of the cobbler's kids having no shoes, but in this case, the cobbler's kids don't have shoes because the cobbler is wearing Gucci slippers for societal traction as he chases some weird illusion of wealth.

I thought I could rise above it—and I did, in many ways. I did good work for my clients and fought for them day in and day out. Though, in hindsight, back then, while I really was taking care of them, I was still fighting for me. I was working hard to make money for myself. Regardless, I gave up more than one sizeable bonus to do the right thing as my colleagues were given accolades and bonuses for what I considered unethical. But there comes a day when you wonder what you are fighting for.

The only way I could compete was to work harder. I was so determined to be successful that I was the first one in and the last one out, hardly realizing my daily routine was making me feel less human. My nickname was "night shift," because I would arrive at the office at five a.m.

# EPIPHANIES FOUND IN THE SILENCE

It wasn't until I was quiet and purposefully processing what was happening around me, and how I'd got to this place, that I realized that how this loss of humanity and compassion had led to some dark places.

My life felt empty. When I got home from work, I ate too much and drank more than the healthy, prescribed one glass of red wine. I almost never slept the entire night through and woke in a cloud. I had a hard time relating to others and very little of my free time was spent interacting with others. As I've said, I didn't have many real close friends.

I'd been so determined to be successful that I'd forgotten my original definition of success. I was caught up in the game, living within the rules of a toxic, greedy culture. When I looked around, I saw many of my colleagues were just like me: shells of human beings with an outward appearance of wealth, but internally—sometimes even financially—broken.

My Volvo moment was not just a moment. It was the awakening I never knew I needed. It allowed me to stand at the mountain top and look around. It allowed me to consider my life choices.

I decided to transition from the mountain to the seas. Sailing, comfortable with being lost, aimless. No apex to climb, just blue on blue. I became the sailor who stops midvoyage, discarding my original motivations to set sail. I needed to find a new motivation or turn the ship around. I could see myself clipping along on a thoughtless path toward riches and isolation, but

I did not know how to connect money and fulfillment.

I sat there, listening but unable to speak. In my forced silence, I began an internal dialogue on what was important to me. Eventually, this experience allowed me to let go, to shed layers, to get back to my purpose, get back to myself.

Slowly, gradually, I began to realize I had never really connected money and fulfillment. I thought back to my days of helping to open the new school in Cairo. Crossing the Nile on my way to work, seeing poverty on the streets every single day. I took this experience and grew from it. I'd moved on to teach the children of elite families in Lebanon and Brazil, talking about the importance of connecting with all classes of people, ending poverty for everyone. Increasingly, I came into contact of the poorest of the poor in those countries through volunteer work or courses on human rights. I volunteered in the favelas (slums) of Sao Paulo, befriended farmers in the landless movement, and eventually took my entitled students to these places to learn from those less fortunate. All the while, I was telling myself I did not need money. Or believed that in some way money was a necessary evil.

But then I moved to Atlanta, and the pendulum clearly swung too far the other direction.

I chided myself for forsaking my first career; I was really good at teaching and it was very meaningful. I had *loved* it. But, God, I hated when people said to me, "Oh, you are a teacher—that must be so rewarding." That is like saying, "Oh, sorry you don't make any money, but you must feel really good about yourself." I didn't want to choose between fulfillment and money security, I wanted both! But in that situation, I was never going to have both.

No doubt, my experience teaching overseas was pleasurable and worthwhile, but it also taught me values and skills, I thought, as I sat in my quiet office.

I learned compassion, how to work with people from all over the world, and meet them where they are at. I learned persistence. Brazilians have an expression, "*Dar um jeito*," which means "To find a way." Nothing is straightforward in Brazil, you need to finagle your way into a solution. That skill became immeasurably important when I started working in large financial institutions—finding legal and ethical solutions to complex client problems in rigid systems is not easy. Here I was now, hoping to solve my own complex problem.

Those photography years I spent in the dark room developing photos translated to my deep unending, often annoying, conviction to process. If you made one mistake in the dark room, you could lose an entire roll of film. The exactitude that was needed to roll a cartridge of film, take the photos, develop the film, and then print the photos was unforgiving. This exacting process alongside the art of actually taking a photo was a contrast and challenge I savored. I looked back on that acquired skill and realized I was letting my creative side die.

Most importantly, I honed in on my superpower, or the one thing I felt I did better than anything else; I have the ability to explain really complicated shit in less than thirty seconds to just about anybody. Was I using this skill to its fullest potential? Probably not.

**The more I sat in silence, I realized I'd been destroying parts of myself, ignoring my value system. Letting skills wither. Ignoring my purpose.**

I wondered if I should just quit financial services. Go back and start over again? But I also wondered if I should try harder at financial services and somehow make it work. Could I bring about the abundance I desired? Not just money, but friendship and connection. Was there passion and purpose in it for me?

# HEALING

It was time to course correct. It was time for healing my present self.

Clearly there was no reason why I couldn't take my values and skills to the world of finance. I "awoke" from my silent meditation and realized that I did not have to reinvent myself. I did not have to quit and move to Tibet, become a schoolteacher again, or spend my entire life working for a charity. All I had to do was find the path that matched my new discovery.

I began to envision myself as much more than a financial advisor doing the work of a large corporation—selling their products, relying on proprietary research, and delivering the firm like a good little lemming. This matched up with my purpose, to serve. I knew eventually I would need to change firms to make this happen. For the time being, though, I would personally take over the management of my client's money and my own money. Even within the confines of my current firm, I could create policies regarding wealth management for my clients that reflected my values and strengths, using a value proposition that was based on abundance—not fear. It was once again a return to myself. Unlike before, where I healed my Money Memory with my past memories, here I was, healing myself in real time by changing how I worked.

Loss can be a great teacher, especially when it forces you to rethink everything you thought you knew about yourself and your career. I set sail once again in search for something more. I examined my personal work practices and fired my third-party money managers, dumped the mutual funds, and completely restructured my how I worked. For starters, these steps brought me closer to the money I was managing, not farming it out to others. I made a conscious decision to start managing risk in a way that supported businesses with a positive impact on society, also channeling my own my money into this force for good.

This was the beginning of a healing process and I was leveraging my career and financial assets—the things that got me in this mess—to get myself out. I was no longer seeing my career or money as something outside of myself, but something within me.

## THE SHIFT

The next thing I did was start asking my clients about their values, to get to know them better and ensure I was not investing counter to their beliefs. I asked them about their Money Memories. I inquired more about my client's goals and made sure our investments were aligned to those goals. And while having these intimate conversations about what mattered most to them, I began to evolve into a trusted advisor. Instead of steering them into one investment product or another, I created a sound, repeatable investment process that was based on empirical data and independent research.

**This profound shift in how I did business made me happier almost immediately. I started asking clients about their children, grandchildren, what mattered most to them, their first Money Memory, estate plans, philanthropy plans. I went from being just a financial advisor to being an indispensable part of their family.**

Every once in a while, I will get a new client who doesn't really know what I stand for and who will call and say something like, "I'd like to pay off my mortgage, but I'm sure you don't agree." The insinuation, in case you don't know, is that I would prefer they invest the money with me rather than for them to live in a house, debt-free. The belief that I would rather make a few bucks instead of serving my clients is hurtful, but I let it go. I don't hold it against them. Our industry is wired that way and people have come to expect it, sadly. If you work at big banks like I used to, you could lose your annual bonus if your clients took money out of the bank to pay down mortgages. I just kindly reply, "I'm always in favor of lowering debt. Of course I want you to own your home outright."

Now, more often than not, my long-term clients will call me after a rough patch in the market and say, "Hey, we are not worried about our investments, but we want to make sure you are OK." That's the type of stuff that makes you cry at the office—the good type of tears. The emotion wells up because they see me, Brandon Hatton. Whether they know it or not, I stopped in the middle of the voyage and recalibrated my reasons for moving forward. I built a business based on my values and my strengths, a business whose purpose was to help others.

The very thing that caused the destruction of my original goal—my career—was the tool I used to heal myself. I began to let go of riches and develop Conscious Wealth. I built a bridge back to myself and a livelihood to continually deepen my understanding of who I am and my place in the world.

I would eventually learn that managing money requires a mix of empathy when working with clients and a lack of emotion with making trades. *This* is the hardest thing about my work. To do it right, I need to be completely attuned to my emotions and what I am feeling so I can help clients better understand what they need; I need to turn off the noise from the news cycle and market volatility and manage investments according to a trading process based on empirical data.

For example, I have had a client call in tears because the market is down and she (unreasonably) believed she would not have enough money because the market is in another one of its crises. Then I had to hang up the phone, bracket that emotion, and trade, potentially into more risk.

This is what I do, balancing behavioral psychology, emotional intelligence and art within a very structured process. Money is emotional and yet the entire world of wealth management is run on responsibility, care, diligence, and exactitude, which is needed when handling and investing money. Yet at the same time, neither we nor our clients are robots.

That particular teary client believed that because the markets were down 30 percent, there was nothing but risk. These clients and even the average investor are investing at the wrong time. And divesting at the wrong time. The truth is, when you take the emotion out of it, that the market is a heck of a lot riskier when it is up 30 percent then when it is down 30 percent.

Finding the best way to serve my clients, to ease their worries and hopefully move them past scarcity issues, has frustrating moments but ultimately it is fulfilling. I have purpose.

# YOUR STORY

I know for me, I needed an experience of loss to heal my money journey (and myself). Silence. Brokenness. The destruction that accompanied my wealth creation allowed me to rebuild where I am today and where I am headed. I changed my story.

Even though it is hard, I invite you to consider all you gave up to get what you have today. What have you given up to create your wealth? Did you start climbing a mountain, like me, to find out it was the wrong one? How many switchbacks did you take along this climb? Or does the sailor analogy work better for you? My truth is that it is difficult to build financial wealth without destroying something, especially the first go-around. If that is true, what did you let go of and should you reclaim it? Is it even worth salvaging?

Once you've lost and gone through destruction, it is time to rebuild. One of the most impactful ways you can do so is through business. You must first heal yourself. Then, you can further that healing through you work. Take a look at the questions below and when you're ready to continue, we will explore business healing in the next chapter.

- Have you had a "Great Volvo Awakening" and what ways did it change your perspective or trajectory of life? Who have you shared this awakening with?
- In what ways has wealth creation caused a separation from your earlier self?
- What losses and destruction have your wealth building or career advancement caused? What have you had to give up?
- How can the losses in your life lead to a rebuild?

CONSCIOUS WEALTH

# LEVEL THREE

# IMPACT

# CHAPTER 6
# HOW CAN WE SHAPE THE FUTURE OF BUSINESS?

**As Jerry Maguire says in his manifesto, "We are losing our battle with all that is personal and real about our business."**

The 1996 movie *Jerry Maguire* generated a lot of great quotes, but this one hits the nail on the head; many of us have lost what is personal and real in our careers, that which originally gave us purpose. For me, my purpose is only deepened when I positively impact others. If you are working toward Conscious Wealth, you, too, will want to consider your business choices and how they impact those around you.

## FOR THE PEOPLE

My grandfather Gus Abood had a supermarket called Abood's Foods. In 1968, he had one of the few stores that was not looted or burned down in the riots that ensued in the aftermath of Martin Luther King Jr.'s assassination. We can never know for sure why his store alone was spared, but family legend holds that the neighborhood respected him. He allowed his customers to ring up essentials like diapers with food stamps. He gave pay advances to his trusted workers. He even sent one of his grocery baggers to the most elite private high school in the city. Talk about conscious business. Gus Abood was a store owner for the people.

## Like my grandfather, good business owners treat their employees like family and are active in their community.

They do not dump trash in a nearby stream because it is *their* stream in *their* community. They know the best way to make a buck is to care about the impact their company has on society and the environment. Society, the environment, their workers' families, the consumers, are all not externalities or consequences of commercial activity that affects other parties. They are all part of the business.

When John Mackey and Raj Sisodia cowrote *Conscious Capitalism* in 2014, they realized that many large and mega-cap corporations had created a lot of wealth for themselves and their shareholders. In doing so, the corporations lost sight of their greater community—their *stake*holders. It is easy to "lose sight" of others when you never actually see them. The corporation's "small town" is the world's population and the "nearby stream" is the environment we all share, but big business often do not see themselves as part of a community, not on a small scale, nor on the larger, worldwide scale.

I read the *Wall Street Journal* and they roundly criticize this evolution of business, even though the Business Roundtable rejected shareholder capitalism in their 2019 letter, stating, "Each of our stakeholders is essential. We commit to deliver value to all of them, for the future success of our companies, our communities, and our country."

Big corporations often claim that the role of business is to maximize profits in the short term but are unwilling to have the real conversations needed to talk about long-term growth creation. There is much more to business than maximizing profits.

Change can be scary, but change is necessary in life, including wealth management. Whatever industry you work in, you can be an agent for change. Work is a reality for just about everybody, but did you know your work is *your* platform to create change? Change for yourself and for your industry. For example, my task is to be a beacon of light or signal for change within wealth management. There are times I feel this industry does not want me, but I continue my work. I know my industry can be kinder and more loving. My industry can be full of businesses that supports the abundance, purpose, and impact of others.

My hope is that you, too, will find healing through your own Money Memory, healing through changing the way you do business, and by challenging your own industry to do better. The next chapter will help you develop your thoughts and an action plan along these lines.

Like me, you may also find healing by challenging your financial advisors and the financial industry. That's

right, if you are here because you have found that being rich isn't enough, that instead you'd like to create
wealth that satisfies your heart as much as your estate,
then you are part of the financial industry, a client at
the very least. Thus, you can be part of change on a
big scale, as a cog in the financial machine. Enough
squeaky cogs can bring about attention to unethical
behavior and hopefully change. This is one way your
business can have a massive beneficial impact on
the world.

# A BRIEF HISTORY OF FINANCIAL SERVICES

This may seem big picture to you, talking about the
history of financial services, but in order for me and
my business to be as successful as possible and have
the biggest positive impact on my clients and community, it's important for me to clarify to myself and
others how the financial service industry works. And
what doesn't work. And why it's so important that I
become involved in fixing it. And urging other service
professionals—and clients—to change how they view
and employ money.

Back in the day, my grandfather had a stockbroker.
If you were around in the second half of the 20th
Century, you may have had one, too, at a company
like Smith Barney, EF Hutton, or Dean Witter. These
names were the keepers of the keys. They had all the
information and access to trade. There was an old
commercial where people are dining at a restaurant
and a guy at one table says to another, "Well, my

broker is at EF Hutton and he says . . ." and the entire restaurant turns silent to listen to his stock tip. Their slogan was *When EF Hutton speaks, everybody listens*. That commercial summed up the relationship between broker and client perfectly.

If you were investing back then, your broker, (or brokers, as many clients had multiple brokers, thinking they could get multiple stock picks), would call you up, give you buy or sell advice, and charge you hundreds or thousands of dollars to broker that trade. If the broker did that enough with the people he knew (clients) and people he did not know (prospective clients who took his cold calls), he made a decent living.

Somewhere in the 1980s, mutual funds became more mainstream and brokers did not have to provide stock tips, but instead, indicated the hottest top money manager who could pick all your stocks in one fund. Even in the eighties, information was not as readily available as it is today. Trading wasn't easily accessible. Thus, these funds often times outperformed the market and provided real value to the client. These funds had pretty big upfront charges—called loads—sometimes as much as 5 percent. Later, they stopped charging front-end loads and had some 2 percent internal fees. Many clients do not know these fees still exist today. The funds also had what we call "trails"—a trailing revenue split to the advisor. So, a broker will sell a client a fund one year and then receive revenue for the entire time the client owned the money, all because of embedded fees that were taken out of the fund on a daily basis. Although it may be surprising, this still occurs today with some advisors.

In the nineties, one mutual fund company grew by leaps and bounds by popularizing a different type of mutual fund that mimicked an index, called indexing. It is not possible to invest directly in an index. These indexing mutual funds provided investors a diverse basket of stocks, but unlike the expensive active mutual fund, the basket rarely changed. Saving money on the expensive rockstar money managers, they became popular very quickly. Because the bulk of them are cheap, transparent, and designed to represent and perform at some slice of the market, they are known to never out- or underperform the market. This gave birth to today's exchange traded fund or ETF. Please be warned that ETFs have evolved since the earliest days and some of the newer generation ones have become much more complex and volatile. Take that for what you will, as this is beyond our conversation at the moment.[5]

Through this evolution, brokers were increasingly expected to provide advice on a myriad of topics, including education planning, retirement planning, social security, long-term care insurance, life insurance, estate planning . . . you name it. The position and title transformed from stockbroker to financial advisor.

The advisor model is better for both the client and the advisor, but since the role is much bigger, the advisor must lean on other experts. No one person

---

[5] Important notes: Investors should consider the investment objectives, risks, charges, and expenses of a mutual fund or exchange traded product before investing. The prospectus contains this and other information and should be read carefully before investing. The prospectus is available from your investment professional.

can do it all. Yet, as we stand today, this transition is not complete, and the industry has work to do.

We can do better. Much better.

# HELP ME HELP YOU

The impact that the financial services professionals are having on the economy, businesses, and on personal lives of individuals is massive. The impact on your business and how it affects others is massive. The responsibilities of these professionals need to be reviewed by everyone at every level, from CEOs to money managers to clients.

In order to mitigate some of the negative widespread impacts, we as an industry first of all need to stop pretending we have advisors who "do it all." A jack of all trades is a master of none. There needs to be more transparency around what your individual advisor actually does and when they lean on experts. For instance, I may know more about insurance, taxes, and estate planning than 90 percent of the general population, but I am not an expert who lives in the minutia. I will always call in the right expert to partner with.

This all may seem like common sense to you, but it is not clearly stated and becomes problematic when you see the implications. In the need to take up more responsibilities, many advisors stopped managing money. This happened for a variety of reasons. For one, firms built out their investment models and offered those models to their advisors, who in turn offer the preset models to the hundreds of thousands of their clients.

**This happened because the firms wanted to scale. Not to spend on training.**

**To make clients sticky.**

**Make advisors sticky.**

**Make money for their shareholders.**

**Commoditize advice. Commoditize advisors. Commoditize clients.**

The firm I run my practice with encourages us to manage money. But before I joined them, I would often be in a conference room with other advisors when former firm officials asked: "Why on earth would you spend your time investing clients' money when we have a team of PhDs in New York who are willing to do your work for you?"

We as advisors were beaten down, made to believe we are incapable of managing money, even though I have a hunch that is the reason most of us got in the business. Many advisors did then become lackadaisical with investing, when the firm would do the bulk of their work for "free" and so decided the easiest way to make more money was to spend their time on gaining new clients. And others gave up the most important part of the job because they just got so overwhelmed with the enormous number of responsibilities the new title "advisor" held.

It is imperative for the client to know who is making the decisions about their money. If you are working with an advisor at one of those big firms named after two men (because that is how they all started), you should know who is deciding what to buy and sell, and when. Some of these firms do not let the advisors manage a dime of the money—it is managed by a central investment team in Manhattan or similar metropolitan area.

As a client, I would want to know who is making the decisions about my money and what is weighing on them. The problem with a boardroom of men and women in a city far away making financial decisions for millions of clients can be illustrated if you think back to the financial crisis of 2008, the negative impacts of which are still resounding today.

Many of these big firms helped cause the 2008 crisis by buying, bundling, and peddling low quality mortgages as safe investments to their clients. In the heat of the crisis, the Wall Street executives were spending sleepless nights in backrooms, scared to death that their firm would go bankrupt, be bought out, or the entire financial system would collapse. They kept their mouths shut. They knew the system was crumbling, yet they did not say a single word to their millions of clients.

I repeat, the leaders of the very banks that caused the financial crisis did not tell their wealth management clients they screwed up because, in part, they were afraid they would lose their jobs and company. They kept millions of clients in their cute little orderly pie chart portfolios while the walls tumbled. That's bullshit! They absolutely did not have the right to withhold such information. To this day, not a single Wall Street executive has gone to jail for that fraud. Not a single company has apologized for withholding vital information to its wealth management clients.

I call for the firms to apologize. The firms and advisors should make it very clear who is making investment decisions and what other factors they have at play. Stop the charade. And I want perspective clients to know they have rights and should be asking: Are you or are you not my advisor? Who manages my money? Is it you or someone in New York City? Is my management plan truly customized or am I just part of the herd? What other considerations do you have when investing money? What is your investment style?

I call on firms to clearly state in writing who is the advisor; is it the firm or the human being who is working with the client? You wouldn't know it, but many of the advisors aren't legally your advisor. The big brokerage houses and firms on Wall Street have legal employment contracts that state the firm is the advisor and the "human being" advisor is there to represent the firm. Even many advisors are in denial of this and many still say "my clients," but know damn well they signed noncompete agreements. If you signed a noncompete, the client belongs to the company.

As a client, do you really want to develop a relationship and work with an advisor who can't leave his or her firm? It's time firms and advisors come clean with the clients. Let the clients know who is managing the money. Who is the advisor, and where/who is that advice actually coming from? Whose interests does this advice serve?

# SHOW ME THE MONEY

I challenge firms to stop incentivizing your advisors to work against their clients. I'm talking about not reducing the advisors' compensation if there is a failure to bring referrals or to provide cross-selling revenue. Advisors shouldn't be paid only if they tie the client to a particular bank and use their time to drive revenue for the bank. The majority of the advisors' time should be spent on what is best for the client. All firms claim they put the client's interest first, and many say there are independent, but in order to really determine who and what a firm is looking out for, you need to follow the money.

The big firms update the advisors' compensation structure on an annual basis. The new compensation structure has been known to come out between Christmas and New Year's Day, when the advisors are on vacation. By design, the structure of pay is meant to influence behavior. These ever-changing compensation structures have traditionally created incentives to send business to the highest-margin divisions or the businesses that are suffering the most. One year, an advisor may need to open ten checking accounts in order to not get dinged on their annual salary. The next year, they may need to sign up six clients to use margin on their accounts or open a new mortgage. I have seen firms require advisors to spend their time bringing in a set number of new accounts instead of taking care of their current clients. Insurance companies that also sell investments are notorious for paying advisors less if they don't sell a certain number of insurance policies.

This is called cross-selling. The banker's credo is *More products make clients stickier.* Yes, clients are routinely called "sticky" in the industry, with the belief they are less likely to leave once you have all your tentacles around them. In theory, this makes sense, but in practice it is dehumanizing. Can you imagine if your hospital followed this credo and penalized your primary care physician for not cross-selling you to other in-house doctors? Ugh, even the words together, sticky and hospital, make me cringe. Yet, it is somehow seen as acceptable and an encouraged practice. It needs to stop.

Compounding the problem of cross-selling and misaligned incentives, some advisors are now being paid part of their salary in ten-year vesting stock of the company. Not a bonus; their previous salary was cut and they are now being paid partially with stock. The problem with this is not only do they get paid less if they refuse to cross-sell, but the value of their stock goes down if they don't. It increases the pressure to sell product instead of serve the client.

When Maguire said, "We are losing our battle with all that is personal and real about our business," he was revealing a problem but goes on to offer hope. We are not doomed to a financial system that grinds up everyone involved. There are solutions. I propose compensation of advisors be consistently transparent and aligned with a sustainable, humanizing advisory practice. That does not mean we should forbid bringing in experts and exposing our clients to the valid offerings of the institution. But penalizing advisors for not selling the firm's products creates a serious moral hazard and undermines the trust we as advisors need to cultivate to do our job.

What does that look like in practical terms? An advisor is compensated by a set percentage of the revenue that his or her practice ethically creates in the best interest of the client. Period. Full stop. No pushing or pulling the advisor to meet a company's goals. Just allowing advisors to do their job and share in the revenue that a successful practice creates. This creates trust. And that trust is stickier than any products.

# WE LIVE IN A CYNICAL WORLD

The battle for care on a personal level that Maguire describes didn't come about in a void. Early in the century, the investment process of Ivy League college endowments was all the rage. They had diversified out of US stocks and bonds and bought into other nontraditional assets such as timber, metals, and real estate. They hired expensive (and successful) outside managers to buy emerging market and international equities. They bought into alternative investments like venture capital firms and hedge funds to use leverage and operate in dark pools. The theory was that they could tie up some of their money in illiquid investments and over the long run perform better because these assets were not publicly traded. That, and their performance had little correlation to US stocks and bonds. The approach was very successful running up until the financial crisis, with outperformance of the general market for years.

Books were written about it, accolades given, and

it inspired much of today's investing for larger institutions. Around that time, you started hearing a lot more about "alternative" investments, meaning any financial investment not stock, bond, or cash. At this time, the financial services industry saw a marketing opportunity and claimed that all investors should invest like the institutions. Or, a more obscene marketing tactic: they should invest like "smart money" does, the implication being that you are dumb if you don't use complex, nontransparent, and illiquid investments.

This push for retail investors to embrace institutional-style investing created an entire line of absurd mutual funds and managed futures products, and permeated the models of these big firms. I have seen portfolios with as little as $100K have alternative mutual funds in them. These mutual funds utilize leverage, take bets on currency and gold, and attempt to perform independently from the main asset classes. Advisors brag they "zig" when your portfolio "zags." I shake my head as I write that expression, because, historically, they have underperformed in up markets and at times completely failed in down markets. The hedge fund and private equity industry took this opportunity to enlarge their reach and started reducing minimums from $10MM to $250K. Even today, you have private investors pushing for their hedge funds to be available on 401(k) platforms.

The issue is not the efficacy of *some* alternative investments. In fact, I love business models and love to invest in innovative businesses that private equity brings to the forefront. What I am saying is, it is the Wild West out there. The character of a fund's General

Partners is equally important to the quality of the investment strategy. An awful lot of due diligence is needed to get it right. What is at issue is the way the "institutional" model is being marketed and misrepresented. You can go to an Ivy League's endowment site today and see that this model has outperformed the broad market indexes over the last decade, but some big details are left out when this is marketed to the retail investor. For starters, this model out performs over time because it is run on leverage, yet the returns are compared to nonleveraged indexes, like the SP500.

During the 2007/8 financial crisis, many of these alternative investments invoked their "gating" provisions and did not let their clients take their money out. There was a lot of smart money trapped in these funds while both families and institutions had real liquidity needs. Compounding the issues is that many of these funds worked off leverage and lost their lines of credit to borrow money. With a loss of the line of credit overnight, they had to dump assets at low prices and some even closed up shop. In the worst of the financial crisis, when these assets were expected to shine, the highly-touted institutional investing model left many investors, including the most famed Ivy League Endowments, performing the same or worse than the general market.

All of this is very problematic for the retail investor. First and foremost, the average client is not an institution. Institutions have hundreds of millions of dollars, will live on forever, are run by educated investors and can rather easily raise more capital. An "average" investor is different. They will not live forever and have real needs for their capital. A couple who retired with, say, $10MM needs that money to be liquid and available so they can live the lifestyle they want. They may want to redo the kitchen, but they don't need to build a dining hall with it. Unlike institutions that have donors, they may not have more money coming in, needing to live off the income and gains from their portfolio. And although intelligent, they may be ill-equipped to understand the complexities of the products that institutions invest in.

We all know the retail investor, with perhaps $50MM in investable assets or less, has less pricing leverage, too. Although they may qualify for such investments, replicating the cost structure of these institutional-style portfolios is usually out of reach. Yet, it is still marketed as a way to get better returns. As an industry that is increasingly becoming commoditized, we need to prove our value as an advisor by more than the returns we can get through expensive, leveraged, out-of-reach institutional model.

Effective communication is the value proposition here. A good return on investments is table-stakes for any advisor—it's not what makes us unique. Let's not democratize illiquid long-term investments with fear-based marketing, not when the basis for Conscious Wealth is transparency. Frankly, the basis of my industry should be trust. When working with families who have institutional-sized assets, good returns is expected. But it should also be expected that we are finding ways for people to use their money to create cohesiveness within their families and their businesses. To be more loving and kinder within. And to connect globally in such way as to make a positive impact.

# THE PURPOSE OF WEALTH MANAGEMENT

The purpose of wealth management is not to make rich people richer. The purpose of our business is to facilitate investing so our clients can live a life of abundance, purpose, and impact.

## The purpose of wealth management is to make the world a better place.

The lack of transparency, compensation structure, malaligned incentives, and the manner of our marketing of products is a real threat to our potential. This business has always been a lucrative business and historically the individual advisor was able to amass wealth by practicing properly over multiple decades. Not so long in the past, brokerage firms allowed their advisors to manage their books of business without artificial ethical constraints placed on them by firms. The advisor served the client, not the bank. Many a firm was content with the slow and steady advisor business, and clients prospered in this model.

We can return to this model with more transparency, decentralization of investment process, ultimately ending compensation practices that value the firm's bottom line over the client's financial future. We can market investments that fulfill our clients' real needs in a way that demonstrates dignity. Who's with me?

The purpose of wealth management is not simply to make money. Well, okay, that is absolutely part of it, but the larger purpose of wealth management is to support individuals and families to become more loving and generous human beings. The way we comport ourselves as an industry can reduce the conditions that lead to fear, scarcity, and hoarding. Moreover, we can create the conditions that lead to an abundant mindset, a purpose-driven life, and generous spirit. Fortunately, these conditions are easily available through transparency, client/advisor-aligned compensation structures, and communication that begins out of respect for the client.

It boils down to this: the industry is fear-based and has little interest in love and healing. I would like to inspire the industry to operate on all levels with love and not fear. The impact of big money can be good on a worldwide scale, just as how you disperse your personal wealth can provide beneficial impacts, so why not move for change?

## SPENDING QUALITY TIME WITH YOUR ADVISOR

There are ways you can help my industry, which in turns helps you, and the world's economic health. You can ask your advisor the following questions:

- Do you have short-term sales goals? What are they?
- Do you get penalized for not cross-selling?
- How do you make money? (follow-up question; How else?)
- Who actually makes the investment decisions in my portfolio? Who else are they making such decisions for? What other considerations do they have when making such decisions?

- Will you recommend products proprietary to your firm? If yes, why?

The answers I would want to hear from my advisor, regardless of their firm, are as follows:

**My compensation is consistently structured in a way that it is in my financial best interest to serve my clients.**

**My compensation is consistently structured in a way that it is in my clients' financial best interest to serve my clients.**

**I get compensated based on the revenue that is generated annually by my clients in a clear, concise manner.**

**I don't have short-term sales goals.**

**I don't get penalized for a failure to cross-sell you to other parts of my enterprise.**

**I don't get penalized or rewarded for using proprietary products.**

**I am not subject to annual compensation structures revisions that push and pull me to increase profit for my company.**

**I am here to serve you. If I do that right, then everything will work out just fine.**

# YOUR STORY

I challenge you to ponder the purpose of *your* industry and write a manifesto for your industry. And if you feel brave enough, publish it.

In order to begin assessing your own business, its purpose in the world, and its impact, consider the answers to these questions.

- Does my company/industry elevate humanity? Consider asking your colleagues.
- Am I selling a product or am I adding value?
- What are the externalities in your work? In your life?
- Write a statement of gratitude around your work.

# CHAPTER 7
# HOW DO YOU MANAGE THE FINANCIAL ADVISOR IN YOUR HEAD?

**The less energy you lose on money from anxiety and angst,** the more energy you will have available to be an agent of healing for yourself, your community, and your industry. Despite the reform that is needed in financial services, there are a great deal of highly qualified and principled advisors out there serving their clients. You may decide to work with one. Or you may decide to manage your own investments. Regardless, even more important than anything else is managing the financial advisor in your head. This is where a solid, consistent process for investing really matters.

## BREAK THE PARALYSIS

Let me tell a story . . . even though it will make me look like an ass. But it's necessary, to show you how important it is that you wrangle that internal financial advisor into submission. I'm telling the story for the sake of transparency and vulnerability and as a way to illustrate tried and true investment principles that support abundance, purpose, impact, and, eventually, unity (which we will be getting into soon).

I hate sleeping on my mistakes. For a guy like me who loves to obtain knowledge and get to the bottom of an issue, even buying a mattress can be an incredible hassle.

One problem of living overseas for so long is that I developed in vastly different ways compared to people my age back in the states. For example, I went through an entire decade never watching a Super Bowl or an episode of *Sex and the City* or *Friends*—and survived! I also never purchased a home or had to fill that home with things, like a matched set of dishes or a mattress. I pretty much rolled into fully furnished apartments my entire adult life and accepted what the landlord had given me.

Even though I consider myself an intelligent guy who can make a decision rather quickly, I found myself sleeping on a mattress shaped more like a parallelogram than a rectangle. It sloped in the middle so badly that I rolled down into the low spot like a Hot Wheels car in a bathtub. This had been going on for a year until my girlfriend warned me that she would stop spending the night if I didn't buy a real mattress.

It wasn't like I couldn't afford it. I went into the first store, cold, without having done any research, and a salesman came right up.

*Oh, gee, he is my friend,* I thought. *He will help me.*

Like at a wine tasting, he progressively moved up in quality until I was laying on a six- thousand-dollar mattress and convincing myself how I absolutely needed this in my life. When I suggested we go back to the mattresses that cost less than roundtrip airfare and accommodations in Italy, the salesman rolled his eyes and said, "Well, I guess so. But you know you will spend more time on this bed than on any single purchase this year."

This guy knew how to hook me.

"Cut corners on anything else, but not a mattress." He spoke as if reciting a proverb or a fortune cookie.

*Hey, wait a minute, I wonder if I am overpaying for this thing. Maybe I should buy a mattress online!* No, that did not seem like a good idea. How would I know if I liked it? *How about if I just buy directly from the factory? That should be cheaper, right? Oh wait, all these things come from the factory. Even the Mattress Factory has stores. It's not like they are building mattresses in the break room.*

Inside my head, the continued rambling was pure jibber jabber. My internal financial advisor was running in circles.

*What would my ancestors do? Actually, they were goat herders and probably slept on straw. They turned out all right. I know I need to spend money, but how much? Will I buy the memory foam mattress only to learn that it makes me too hot? Or will I buy the conventional mattress with a pillow top and have a ten-year sentence on an outdated mattress? I can see it now. My friends will be bragging about their memory foam mattresses, and I will have to wait until I am sixty to try one. Or maybe I should get a Sleep Number bed. I am not married now, but ten years is not too aggressive of a goal to find a lifelong partner. And what if she doesn't like plush beds? What will I do then? Oh gosh, I wonder if she is a side sleeper. That could throw all my plans off. And, by the way, whatever happened to waterbeds?*

The more knowledge I gathered, the farther I seemed from picking the best answer. The unlimited choices paralyzed me for a year, but lucky for me, my girlfriend hung on. Who would have thought finding the truth about a mattress would be so difficult? I just closed my eyes to the whole thing and slept on an uncomfortable bed because it was easier than making a decision I might regret. Truth be told, I could not bear the thought of being reminded every day for the next ten years of how I made a bad purchase. The part of me who was born and raised in Cleveland, wrestled for three years in high school, and lived pretty Spartan-like overseas, said I could handle any bed or any situation that came my way.

Yet, the driven, goal-oriented part of me kept telling me there was a perfect bed out there. This platonic ideal of a mattress allowed me to search endlessly for perfection while simultaneously taking no action when the mattress did not live up to my ideal. This perfectionism was setting me up for failure. What was scary to me was that the more I did this, the more I seemed to revel in it.

I knew I had to do something. I told myself I could deal with any salesman—hell, I lived in the Middle East for three years and came back with carpets—but I needed to deal with my inner voice first.

I reminded myself there was no single bed that was best for me. There were trade-offs and a spectrum of outcomes from any single purchase. I did not have the luxury of waiting until I found a definitive answer.

I had approximated the truth from reading comments online and from comparison shopping. I had to make a choice based on my knowledge at the given time and move on. Would I regret the purchase one day? Perhaps, but I would not fault myself.

I had done my due diligence and could make an informed decision. Key here is I *did* make a decision and moved on. But why was it so difficult?

Admittedly, the purchase of this mattress was a *mundane* responsibility, a purchase I had to make in order to protect my health and wellbeing. If I am well rested and healthy, I can live another day and take on what really does matter to me. The same applies to the purchase of a home, a career change, or entering or exiting a key relationship. I didn't blindly pick a mattress and hope for the best. Once I got my head screwed on straight, I surrendered to the process, approximated truth, made a decision, and moved on.

## YOUR PSYCHE IS THE WORST FINANCIAL ADVISOR YOU CAN HIRE

All of this relates to your money and investing because there will always be a voice in your head that says you need to do something: *You need to tinker with this portfolio or that holding or sell this sector and buy that sector.*

Few people will just buy something and turn their backs on it. Nor should you. To be clear, I don't believe you can just sit there and "ride" out the market through the peaks and troughs. That's called passive investing and it's not how I'm wired. When I'm investing, I need a plan. The plan must be made with a calm mind and not in the midst of a turmoil. It also must be specific enough so I know when and how to act in the future.

Today's markets move fast! But being too active can also cost you. Using a real-life example, let's say you wake up on January first and you have a news badge on your phone that says: "Dow Future set to open down 200 points, signaling an ugly start for stocks this year." You could rub your eyes, start preparing moves to your portfolio, get out of stocks before everybody else, and be the smartest guy in the room.

Or you can take a breath, slow down, and more reasonably think, "Wait a minute, those are just the futures. The market doesn't open for another two hours. And last Wednesday, the Dow battled back from a 600-point deficit to end the day up 600 points. That is a 1200-point swing in one day. Does this news outlet just think I fell off the turnip truck? The first day of the new year is no indication of how the year performs. This is all just noise. I'm going back to bed."

In this real-life example, US stocks were actually up by double digits a few months later. But that is not the point.

## There is way too much information about the stock markets and investments.

**With way too many people claiming to know the answer, you could delude yourself into thinking the more knowledge you obtain, the more likely you will find a definitive answer.**

One day the market is down 800, and two days later, it is back to where it started. And it takes a week to fully understand what prompted the dip in the first place. It's the conundrum.

Overreact to the market, and you can get whip-sawed. If you don't react, that can get ugly, too. It all sounds too much like my silly mattress example.

## TURN OFF THE TV, UNPLUG FROM SOCIAL MEDIA

The tension of investing is artificially exacerbated by the media. I highly recommend you stay away from using the television or social media to inform any of your investment decisions. Cable financial news is interesting, but, remember, it is entertainment. I think many of us know deep down that CNN and Fox News are more often entertainment than news, but forget too often that cable networks focused on the markets are part of the same animal. They are selling ads all day. If you listen to them on satellite radio, you will hear dozens of advertisements in a single hour. In fact, they were so busy selling ads that they all missed the coming financial crisis of 2007 and 2008, you know the largest crisis since 1929. They were too busy being cheerleaders for the market with the formulaic point-counterpoint framework instead of being actual journalists who scrutinized the fraud in the system.

Now, I will say, many times they have fantastic interviews with some great investors and CEOs, but all the dramatic music, flashing headlines, news teasers and varied-volume tactics are manipulating the audience, meant to create a specific mood, to cause tension, and draw in the listener. But they never dial back the tension, never offer closure to the listener. They don't give you the answers—you know why, right? Because they don't have them, of course!

## Also, do yourself a favor and ignore the guy who said he predicted the last financial crisis.

It is known that if you predict the next crisis, you can one day draw in investors by telling them how smart you are. Paul Samuelson, who said, "The stock market has predicted nine of the last five recessions," would surely extend this to include stock market pundits today. If you hear, "Meet Joe, the guy who predicted the last recession!" you will next hear a call to action, "Call Joe! Send him money or get his free pamphlet on gold coins." There is little damage to the pundit's reputation if they are wrong, but the reward is great.

Understand that there is an incentive to make bold calls, knowing most people will forget them unless you are right. But these "fortune tellers" also know that if for some reason they get the timing of the next crisis, they can use that as a marketing tool for the rest of their lives. And they will brazenly do it on major cable networks.

Fintwit, the investing community on Twitter, is equally hazardous to use for advice on your investment strategy. Twitter is full of people pumping their own stock so others will buy it and raise the price of their stock. I, of course would lose my license for this, but many amateur stock-pundits with far less experience have no barriers or ethical guidelines. Others will spend their energy saying they are shorting a stock in hopes it will go down. None of this is regulated and the claims on Fintwit are hardly audited. There are better ways to research investments than in undocumented, two-hundred-and-eighty-character tweets, oftentimes anonymous. Even more importantly, many people on Fintwit are traders and speculators. That means they are investors for the short term, a valid way to interact with the markets but an entirely different animal than long-term investing.

# YOU CAN'T TIME THE MARKET

Amateur investors who try to *time the market* (otherwise, to "predict" future market movements and then use those predictions to move in and out of the stock market instead of holding onto long-term assets) usually lose money.

The market fosters a cycle of emotions. Since 2008, everybody thinks the first sign of a tremor is the next big one. Definitely do not let the little financial advisor in your head get stuck on this investment strategy. What is tough about timing the market is you need to be right twice—when to get out and when to get back in. This is not easy. Consistency and commitment to process is so much more valuable than timing. The consequences are compounded when you realize that, according to a Putnam Investments report, if you missed only ten of the best trading days—only ten days missed from 2003 to 2018—your SP500 returns would be cut in half! It's just tough to time the market with so much volatility and false signals.

# LET GO OF YTD RETURNS

It's also good to keep in mind that investing is a multiple-year endeavor. That means being concerned about how your account performed in a calendar year compared to one or multiple benchmarks is not very useful. Statistically, it is absolutely meaningless to measure a portfolio for 365-day intervals or at year-to-date.

How would you feel if your financial advisor provided you with returns based on the lunar calendar? I can see it now, "Ah, Mr. Client, your portfolio is up 8 percent via the lunar calendar to date; it took a dip when Saturn eclipsed the moon but has really fought back and I expect to see double digit returns before the vernal equinox."

In all seriousness, the most useful way to monitor your returns is on rolling three-, five-, and ten-year returns.

# REMEMBER, YOU ARE THE BENCHMARK

A common trap for investors is to chase markets and benchmark returns as a way to keep score.

I get it, I live and work in the belly of the beast, an industry of constant comparison. Many investors, and maybe even you, have been trained by to put way too much emphasis on the benchmark. Did I meet the benchmark? Did I exceed it? Underperform? All these questions that people have been taught are so crucial are not really that important. The danger is that they stimulate our fear of missing out (FOMO).

Even if you have a secure and abundant mindset, you may still get that pit in your stomach when your neighbor or the guy at the cocktail party is bragging on how his advisor beats the benchmark all the time. You may wonder, *Oh heck, am I beating the mark? Am I missing out?* When that happens, please consider the following:

Benchmarks are probably the most misunderstood concept in investing. The idea is simple: if you are investing in large companies in US markets, then you benchmark your returns by the SP500, a list of the largest 500 companies in the US. When most people say you can't beat the benchmark, this is the benchmark to which they are referring. What unfortunately happens all too often, is people measure a diversified portfolio of small companies, international companies, emerging market companies (all of which are benchmarks) to one single benchmark, the SP500. That would be like measuring track times of a Porsche 911 to a ride to the grocery store in a minivan with your kid in the backseat. Obviously, one is going to take a lot more risk. The other one just needs to get a gallon of milk and return home safely.

There is value in beating a single benchmark and, yes, it is increasingly difficult today. However, the real value comes from the benchmarks you have exposure to at any given time. Decisions on when to buy more bonds, less bonds, add China, decrease China exposure—these are the real decisions that must be made and provide more value than trying to beat a basket of 500 stocks.

The real value is created in the combination of investments that include assets from all benchmarks, *using a process*, not willy-nilly. The rules-based approach to increasing one or another is based in real time. In other words, having a process to add emerging markets, as an example, and when to avoid them. When to add bonds to a portfolio and when to sell them. That is increasingly more important than trying to buy a set number of stocks that "might" beat a benchmark.

The problem with the fear of missing out on returns, is it drives you to take on more risk, perhaps risk you simply don't need to take. If you don't need to take it, then it is a waste of energy. Energy wasted around something as impermanent as money detracts from what is real—your life. The whole point of money and investing is so you can live a better life, not so you can spend all your time playing risky games.

This is the pinnacle of a Conscious Wealth mindset. Let go of arbitrary benchmarks. If you are an investor who wishes to cultivate a Conscious Wealth mindset, you only have one benchmark: you!

Yes, *you* are the benchmark! You are the one that matters.

**When you know what you need to spend, how much is your "enough," and what type of returns you need from your portfolio to live the life you want, then *that* is the benchmark. That is the return you need. Hone in on that number and allow the rest to go.**

You can't get to the point where you are making a positive impact on yourself, your family, your company, or your community if you don't embrace yourself as the benchmark. The story is all about you. Own it.

# CONSCIOUS WEALTH: THREE PRINCIPLES FOR INVESTING

My process, using three investing principles that have been around since long before the stock market, cultivates a Conscious Wealth mindset. I am about to share a high-level explanation of my process, which I designed for my personal investments and is utilized for my clients' investments—but you should know, this is not the only way to invest. It is, however, the Conscious Wealth way.

The three investing principles upon which Conscious Wealth Management is based:

- The investment is transparent.
- The investment provides confidence.
- The investment provides a predictable cash flow.

As a warning, my process puts these principles into practice, but it is not sexy, overly sophisticated, or modern.

# TRANSPARENCY: KNOW WHAT YOU OWN

Peter Lynch, a well-known investor, once said, "You must know what you own." Nothing could be more true.

This investment principle is key to my process. I know that sounds obvious or perhaps even silly to have to say it, but it is imperative in healthy wealth creation. So many people I meet say something to the effect, "I don't worry about that. My spouse, mother, father, sister, or advisor manages it all for me and I don't care," and that is definitely not healthy.

**I can not rely on someone else to maintain my physical health (no one else can eat vegetables or go running for me), so why would I give away what is ultimately my responsibility in regards to the bottom line of my financial health?**

I must personally be able to pull my financial net worth statement and investment account statements and look at each line item and know what each holding is.

Take this common example. A guy was once referred to me because he was not happy with the returns of his portfolio or with his current advisor. He wanted to see if I could do better. This actually happens quite often, though I am generally pretty cautious in such a scenario for several reasons. The advisory relationship is a relationship with trust at its core.

If you are leaving your advisor to work with me because they don't communicate well, they have an inferior service model, or you don't think they are a good fit—let's talk. But if you are leaving a relationship for no other reason than you don't like your returns, you will inevitably leave my team the day we happen to underperform your expectations.

Nevertheless, I met with him and listened. What I discovered was that his returns were acceptable, but the client was still pretty anxious. After digging a bit deeper, I learned that his discomfort came from his inability to see that he had enough money to reach his goals. When he looked at his statements, all he saw was investment products that did not mean anything to him. They had names like Fealty Core Alpha Russell International Small Cap Fund[6], an unknown entity with a mouthful for a name. So, we performed a portfolio analysis based on his statements.

What we discovered was for $10MM in assets, he had thirty funds. Within these thirty funds, he had a

---

6   This name is fictionalized.

total of 25,000 underlying investments. His average investment size was $400. Throughout his entire investing life, he'd been told he needed to be diversified to keep him safe. But he sure did not feel safe. He had no idea what he owned. With so many positions, it was hard to understand why his portfolio was up or down, which was partly why there'd been a lack of communications around his returns. With so many positions, it would be difficult to accurately adjust to market conditions. It was no wonder he was anxious. He went back to his advisor, armed with information and knowledge of how our process led to transparency. Eventually, however, he landed back with us—our process resonated with him.

I operate on the premise that you can diversify a domestic large cap portfolio with thirty stocks, and that every stock you add after that only makes your investment portfolio the slightest bit less risky. Owning shares of a company is called direct investing. It is the most transparent way to invest. Whenever possible, I do this. I own actual shares of companies so that when I look at my investment statement, I see companies' names that I know.

I have a process, based on the Conscious Wealth Management framework, to determine how many I hold at any given time, what sectors are represented at any given time, and under what conditions I buy and sell these stocks. I do the same thing for bonds. This is called direct investing and it is king in my process. There are times I use financial products (funds) because that market is too risky to buy directly, but the bulk of my portfolio is always directly owned and therefore transparent.

# TRANSPARENCY: ADVANTAGES

Transparent direct investing has some real practical advantages. For starters, it allows you to accurately adjust a portfolio when needed. In order to effectively manage the risk of a portfolio, it is really important to know when you are buying, holding, and selling an investment. It is impossible to know what will happen in all your funds on any given day. One fund may change their holdings one day while another changes it the next. Accurately adjusting your exposure to companies and sectors is paramount and more difficult to do with indirect investing.

Beyond the transparency for the client in direct investing, I find that, for myself, owning companies directly gives me a peace of mind: I am investing in a company, its product, its vision for the future, its leadership team, its approach to its stakeholders. That is a dramatically different mindset than if I am investing in the stock market. The stock market may be up or it may be down, but I'd be damned if I knew the reason half the time. There are times it takes us weeks to understand why the markets responded a certain way on a certain day. I go to bed not really caring what the market does, I am more interested in what my companies will do. If it is March and we are starting a pandemic and my portfolio is down 15 percent, I don't wonder where the market will be in December. I look at my companies that I have ownership in and wonder, will they make it? That is a big mindset difference.

# CONFIDENCE: KNOW WHY YOU OWN IT

Peter Lynch followed up his famous quote about knowing what you own with "... And why you own it." As I look at my statement and see a list of companies' names and bond issuers that I know, the confidence in my investment comes from knowing the business. I am able to do research or purchase research on their strategy, strategic advantages, assets, or debt. I am able to listen to the CEO and listen to their vision for the company. I am able to read their financial statements, listen to earnings calls, and make a rational decision on whether to buy it, based on empirical facts. I use written rules and guidelines to make and enact those decisions.

**This is the second principle: I have confidence in the company where I am putting my money. I know why I own it and why I will sell it.**

Beyond financial, there is also the ethical reason for knowing what companies are in your portfolio. In that first discussion with the man I mentioned earlier, the one who was unhappy because he didn't know what he owned, I asked him, "Are you aware that you hold Facebook in three of your funds?"

He said, "No, I hate Facebook."

The impacts of your investment choices are real. When you support a company you believe in, both financially and in the way they interact with the community, you are putting your money where your mouth is . . . at least you hope you are. Again, transparency is key. Is your money invested in companies with a solid vision for the future? Or are you like this guy, who unknowingly invested in a company he would not have chosen to support?

The scope of this book does not permit me to explain how I buy and sell and under what conditions, but what is important is, like me, you have a specific process, and it is written down. In the case you are working with an advisor, you should better understand what their process for choosing and acting on investments entails. If you are investing on your own, at the very least you should have a written investment policy statement that is reviewed on specific dates.

A nonexhaustive list of questions that your investment policy statement should address:

- How will I determine my asset allocation? Will it be strategic or more active?
- Under what conditions will I buy?
- Under what conditions will I sell?
- How often will I review my holdings?
- How often will I make trades?
- How often will I rebalance my portfolio so that it returns to the intended allocation?
- What is my investment philosophy? How often will I review the written version of this?
- How will I measure risk?
- Where will I document this?
- Who will keep me accountable?
- What is my investment philosophy? Where is it written?

# PREDICTABLE: KNOW YOUR NUMBERS

The third principle in investing is finding predictable investments that will provide a cash flow, which means you will find yourself embracing the good old principles of math. Math is certainty. It doesn't waver. So many investment portfolios are designed to grow for some magical day in the future, but the obvious is that you can't count on the future alone.

**You need exposure to investments that are more predictable and have cash flow now in a certain way. High quality fixed income contracts, such as CDs, treasury, municipal, and investment-grade corporate bonds can add more certainty to your portfolio.**

Investing for a cash flow is complex, but the common thread is that all of these "fixed" investments have a purchase price, a price you get at a certain date, and income you receive along the way. For example, if you buy a $100 face value bond at $100 with a ten-year maturity with a 3.5 percent coupon rate, then you will get 3.5 percent of $100 for *every year* and, at the end of ten years, you will receive the face value of $100. The price of the bond may be worth $85 or $105 dollars, along that ten-year time horizon, but if you just hold it and the issuer is able to make good on its loan, you will not lose money. It's no sure thing, but it is the closest thing to certainty we have in the investment world.

Bonds are considered "fixed income" because the amount you receive from them is fixed every year. It is an agreement between one borrower (the company or government) and the lender (the investor). If you buy a ten-year treasury bond, you have an agreement with the United States Treasury that they will pay you back in ten years and also pay you a fixed amount of interest every six months. If you plan on holding that bond until its maturity, you really don't care what happens to its value. You may buy that bond and the dollar can get downgraded, interest rates can go up, and hell can freeze over, but as long as the US is paying its obligations in ten years, you have a predictable source of income and reliable cash flow.

Bonds stop becoming "fixed" income once they are wrapped together in an investment product like a mutual fund or ETF.[7] You never actually own a bond when you own the fund, you just own an indivisible portion of their entire portfolio. The fund is buying and selling bonds on a daily basis for a variety of reasons, including to adjust the yield, credit quality, or to free up money from other investors who are selling the bond. Therefore, there is no fixed maturity date—a date when the loan term you provided is up. You have no idea what this fund will be worth in ten years because you don't own the contract/bond. Your yield—the amount you receive as income—is constantly changing. It can go up or down dramatically. It is very hard to plan. It

---

7    Bond prices and yields are subject to change based upon market conditions and availability. If bonds are sold prior to maturity, you may receive more or less than your initial investment. Holding bonds to term allows redemption at par value. There is an inverse relationship between interest rate movements and bond prices. Generally, when interest rates rise, bond prices fall and when interest rates fall, bond prices generally rise.

ETF shareholders should be aware that the general level of stock or bond prices may decline, thus affecting the value of an exchange-traded fund. Although exchange-traded funds are designed to provide investment results that generally correspond to the price and yield performance of their respective underlying indexes, the funds may not be able to exactly replicate the performance of the indexes because of fund expenses and other factors.

**Investors should consider the investment objectives, risks, charges and expenses of an exchange traded product carefully before investing. The prospectus contains this and other information and should be read carefully before investing. The prospectus is available from your investment professional.**

is hard to know what you can count on. It is incredibly challenging to invest with bond funds for capital preservation. On top of that, you are paying an extra layer of expenses for something that could have been purchased directly. Captain Obvious here: I would not consider this a predictable investment.

# LET'S DECREASE THE NOISE

An investor is more likely to cultivate abundance and purpose if they have some level of comfort with their investments. If they are able to know what they own, why they own it, and understand what they can reasonably expect in terms of cash flow. If they can bridge the gap created by excessive financial products, synthetic benchmarks, and the endless voices making a livelihood in creating FOMO, jealousy, and discomfort.

All the discomfort caused by not knowing for sure what will happen may not go away, of course. The only way to deal with discomfort is to sit with it and let it takes its course. Much like I did with my Money Memory and the realities of my career and lifestyle after the Great Shitty Volvo Moment. But for the love of Peter Lynch, I don't need to add to the discomfort. Indeed, I can invest in a certain way and create a process that decreases the noise. In turn, this increases my ability to sit with the discomfort.

**My task when investing is not to avoid risk. Nothing will achieve that for me. Thank goodness. Without risk is certainty. Certainty is boring. And certainty does not allow for innovation or growth.**

The purpose of my investing process is to create enough certainty so that you can take risks in other parts of your portfolio, and moreover, your life. Because indeed, all this discomfort is not real. It's just allowing yourself to be uncomfortable but calm in moments of uncertainty. When the stock market is tanking, when your bond has been downgraded, or when the talking head on TV is spouting about the missed opportunity on the next high-flying stock, stop, breathe. Ask yourself: how can I learn to sit with the discomfort?

I moved to Atlanta to find work with determination and vulnerability. I took positive steps toward creating more certainty and at the same time, I knew I could not control the outcome of my move. Like many who came before me and most probably you, I took a chance in a new place and found a thrill in the unknown.

Nowadays, I acknowledge and am grateful for uncertainty. Some days it creates a buzz in my stomach. Other times, it just nags at my chest until it is recognized. It is the same physical sensation of excitement. Excitement, adventure, and possibility are good. If the spectrum is between vulnerability and security, I strive to be as far away from security as possible on any given day and constantly pushing it. I play it safe enough with my finances and business so that I don't have to play it safe in life.

That mattress I bought turned out terrible after eighteen months and the warranty was designed to never really go into effect. I ended up giving the mattress away to the movers. All that effort and I still made the wrong decision. And that's okay. I learned a lot and began the process again. The next time it went much smoother.

I walk through life now knowing I'm never going to get everything right all the time—not in the markets or in my personal life—even with all the knowledge in the world. Knowledge is only meant to approximate the truth, not find it. So, as I gain more knowledge and this new information becomes evident, I approximate truth. And when that truth is approximated, I make decisions from a higher ground. And then on and on it goes, as time moves forward and more knowledge becomes available, I am able to adjust my course of action or inaction from my newly approximated truth. And this cycle between knowledge, approximation of truth, and action is what I do. And I do it deliberately and with compassion.

# BUILDING YOUR SPECIFIC STRATEGY

There are indeed independent research firms out there that do not make money off ads, but by paid subscriptions to their data and analysis. This independent data, preferably multiple points, is essential when making your investment strategy.

One of the first documents we prepare with a potential client is an Intersection Report. We use the collected information to begin to wrap our arms around their financial picture, including a complete list of what people own and allocation. Asset allocation is one of the biggest drivers of risk and important to have clarity on. This type of clarity is essential to help them see what they own and why the own it. There is a sample Intersection Report at the end of this chapter, and I highly recommend you fill it out.

Other factors in creating a financial plan investment strategy include these considerations:

**How will I determine my asset allocation? Will it be strategic or more active?**

**Under what conditions will I buy?**

**Under what conditions will I sell?**

**How often will I review my holdings?**

**How often will I make trades?**

**How often will I rebalance my portfolio so that it returns to the intended allocation?**

**What is my investment philosophy? How often will I review the written version of this?**

**How will I measure risk?**

**Where will I document this?**

**Who will keep me accountable?**

**What is my investment philosophy? Where is it written?**

As you answer these questions and build out a strategy, you will have a process. Of course, none of this is guaranteed to always provide you with the right answer. There is a spectrum of outcomes at any given time. The investment process, like the mattress purchasing process, is not intended to find the truth. It is intended to approximate the truth. And the process keeps us disciplined. Discipline is knowing when to act and when not to act. All we can do is control the controllable. Once that is done, we are free to pursue purpose, growth, and other things that really matter.

# YOUR STORY

Let's return to your story. Take a moment to reflect and write your answers to these questions:

- After considering strategies and processes, how do you feel about the opposing statements:

  *The universe will provide. If it's meant to be, it will happen.*

  And:

  *The devil is in the details. If I am detailed enough, I can control the outcome.*

- Do you throw money at uncertainty? Do you know what you own and why you own it? Does it give you more confidence?
- After filling out the Intersection Report below, were there any surprises? Were you aware of all that you own?

# AN INTERSECTION REPORT: UNDERSTAND WHAT YOU OWN AND WHY YOU OWN IT

You can do this with your advisor, or you can do it on your own. But please do it.

Know what you own and why.

## Page 1

Carefully list all land, business, investment accounts, insurance policies, et al.

1. List all of your assets.
2. List all of your liabilities.

## Page 2

Create an overall asset allocation.

1. Stocks
2. Bonds
3. Cash
4. Alternatives

## Page 3

Create a list of all the underlying assets.

1. List underlying assets within investment products. These can usually be obtained on the fund's web page.

# CHAPTER 8
# WHAT IMPACT DO I (AND MY MONEY) WANT TO MAKE?

**My family argues a lot.** As I mentioned earlier, I explored the world from the time I was twenty-one until I was thirty-three to get away from the tension. When I did come back, I quickly learned I was not cut out for the big holidays with my family and so arranged my schedule to come home only for Thanksgiving and the Fourth of July. After all, I thought, the tension and pressure had to be less when we weren't dealing with the birth and death of Christ on Christmas and Easter. Well, I was wrong. Any celebration labored under unresolved issues, which created tension every time my family was around each other. We really needed a reset button.

After a few years of me being back in the US and avoiding Christmas, my father unveiled his sharpest weapons to get me home—guilt and my mother. He successfully planned a surprise retirement party for my mom close enough to Christmas that I would have to stay for the holiday or look like a real jerk. I set aside my plans to go to a tropical island and started working toward finding a domestic flight and the right mindset to head to Cleveland in December.

Growing up, we always had *Better Homes and Gardens* lying around the house. My mom loved looking at the gardens—as a matter of fact, she is so amazing at arranging flowers, we could wallpaper the living room with blue ribbons. Anyway, I would see families in this magazine laughing, sitting carefree on a porch swing, or making cheers with ice tea under an umbrellaed table. I would think to myself, *Yep, that is a better home.* Over the years, I have met families that truly do love each other and know how to display it. I have friends, colleagues, and clients who cannot wait to get home and hang out with their family. They want to vacation with them. They want to go on walks together and just sit around a campfire and talk about life. We as a family, however, only got the first one right—we loved each other, but we did not know how to show it, at least for a long time.

So, another time when I realized I was expected to be at home for a holiday gathering, it popped into my head that I could hold a family conference call instead. *Genius*, I thought. *Absurdity*, one friend informed me. He asked me how it was possible that a grown adult could not already know how it was important to spend time with family they had not seen in six months. He was from a *Better Homes and Gardens* family. I ignored him and moved ahead with my plan.

The first thing I did was call my mom, dad, and sisters individually. I stated the problem as I saw it. "Hey sis, when I come home, it seems like people are arguing the entire time and it puts me on edge. I end up feeling pretty sad about the whole thing." I told her I was holding a family meeting to discuss how we felt about the holidays together and I wanted her to attend. She accepted the invite and I prepped her with the three-question agenda:

1. How does the ideal holiday look to you?
2. What would it require from you?
3. What would it require from others?

I then had the exact conversation with my mom, dad, and my other sister. These conversations were met with resistance and disbelief by some, but also approval by others. When the day had come to hold our family meeting—which we actually did hold over the phone, since we were in different cities—everybody had been thinking about their expectations for the holiday and came prepared.

One by one, we spoke and listened to one another. We heard each other's concerns and stated our own. It was a constructive conversation. But what really surprised me was that what we had said on the phone actually translated into action. We went ahead with the family holiday, in person, but it was much smoother. My sister, for example, did not sleep on the couch, which happened to annoy an early bird like me. I did not go overboard making the meal, which in the past may have added stress to other family members. For a brief moment, we took a "holiday" from our gripes and had a really good time. Far and away, it was the best Christmas our family had experienced up until that point. There was an awareness of each other's expectations and we worked to uphold them.

A few days after I returned home, I received a handwritten note from my mother. I cried as I read it. She wrote a heartfelt message, thanking me for a great Christmas. As I stood in my driveway, reading, I realized I was no longer the hapless kid in the living room hoping everybody would stop arguing. I had always tried to be the peacekeeper growing up, but I did not have the tools or sense of authority to be effective. I could now stand up and influence my life and my family dynamic. I also realized the remarkable power of setting an intention.

**It all starts with stating what you want, and you can have an impact on the outcome.**

## OH HONEY, THAT IS A FAMILY MATTER

The most effective and cohesive families are the ones who set intentions as a unit. They have a written document—a one-pager—that states who they are as a family and what they stand for. I call this one-pager a Family Matters Statement because when I once proposed it to a family in Georgia, the matriarch of the family said, "Oh honey, that's family matters." A Family Matters Document has at least three sections: values, family vision, and world vision.

In the first section, the family lists their values, usually no more than five words like "integrity" or "compassion." The family vision section states how they want to be as a family unit in the world. It contains goals and family guidelines. For example, the head of the family might have the goal to retire at age sixty and continue to work on passion projects and support younger entrepreneurs. Another goal might be to travel annually as a family. There can also be a social media policy for the family, or conditions on how family money is used to support individual educational expenses and business endeavors. Family governance issues can be outlined, like who gets to work in the family business, and how much time and education is needed before taking over certain divisions or taking on certain responsibilities.

The final section is aspirational. It states what type of world the Smith's dream of living in. It says that if all things were possible, how would you like the world to be? These three sections are revisited at least annually. They serve as a guide for family decisions related to just about everything, including vacation, investment policy, philanthropic strategy, a home purchase, college funding, and business succession.

# WHY ARE YOU YELLING AT ME? I'M NOT YELLING, YOU ARE . . .

This simple, one-page document can change everything.

Families can get stuck in a cycle of unproductive or destructive communication. It can range from the annoyance of bickering to the destruction of shouting matches. If you are the person in your family who has created financial wealth, maybe, like me, you climbed the wrong mountain, worked on healing yourself and your relationship with money, and are living a life of abundance and purpose. Well, the most obvious next step is that you want your family to have all that, as well.

You want your family to live in harmony. You want your spouse to enjoy his or her definition of success. You want your children to live not your life, but the highest and most authentic expression of who they are. Most of all, you want them engaged—engaged in anything productive will most often do the trick. You certainly want them to be engaged in the family but also pursuing their own dreams. Perhaps they are already there alongside you and always have been, but a rift occurred during the wealth creation stage, making it hard to see.

The process of writing a Family Matters Document is part of the healing. It brings the family together in spirit and person. It opens doors to communication and understanding. It is inclusive in nature. It can create a sense of fairness by establishing rules and guidelines for wealth distribution, which can reduce resentment and passive aggressiveness. By stating what the family is going to "be" and what a family will "do" in the world, the agreement creates harmony. And without harmony, you can forget about anything else.

# A NORTH STAR FOR DECISION MAKING

Every major well-known US company has a mission and value statement. Board members and CEOs pull out those strings of words whenever they are considering an acquisition or major decision. Yet, I have found these same individuals most often go home to a void of written guidelines. It's interesting that family coherence strategies are ignored, while an incoming CEO would not dream of operating a business without a written and defined culture. They know that each decision that comes before the board will be debated endlessly without such a statement. It's very possible the CEO would enter into endeavors and markets that dilute their mission if the mission was not clearly defined. The employees would be less motivated because they would not understand their part in the greater purpose of the company. And the leadership may indeed be resented because he/she would make decisions that appear to be from the hip, or worse, "unfair."

A stated purpose can unify the hundreds of thousands of people working all over the world and allow a company to thrive. Families, on the other hand, don't need mission statements because of their scale. Even my big Lebanese family with my countless uncles and cousins is not *that* big. Families don't have scale, but if you've ever been in one, you know they have complexity—families do need a Family Matters Document, because of that complexity and the history. Most importantly, families have an ability to make a strong impact and that should be addressed. All of these are factors begging for a written one-pager. A north star to guide decisions.

## INVESTMENT POLICY

The money you invest impacts the world, without question. Your money works on your behalf and can heal or harm others. Investing is an opportunity to further your positive impact in the world. It is an opportunity to continue your healing by allowing others to heal. If you are investing, you absolutely need an investment policy. Investment policies are traditionally tailored to two factors: family's "needs" and risk tolerance. Yet, for the family that has written what they stand for, they can allow their investments to further their values, their purpose and their vision for the world; an investment policy can be tailored to increase their impact in the world.

As I write, I know this type of investing can be extremely complex to understand. The problem is the industry itself has not decided on a universal lexicon to define investing that simply seeks *more than* short-term profit. A lot of words like *sustainable investing; environmental, social, and governance (ESG); green investing; impact investing; and double bottom line investing* are used interchangeably. The scope of this book is not to debate what words to use, but I will define them the way that I and a great many of people in the field do. The following also contains a roadmap to incorporating your vision and values into your investment strategy for maximum impact.

# ROADMAP TO INVESTING TO MAKE A DIFFERENCE

Here is the first step: exclude any investment that works against your family values. This is quite easy to do if you are investing directly in companies and products—just don't invest in them. The cynic might say that excluding investments does not make a difference, and, heck, the Rockefeller Family Foundation did divest themselves of all oil stocks and Exxon did not flinch. The point here is not necessarily to make a difference in that company, but to make sure you are not investing in something you don't believe in.

**If you have a vision for the world that is greater than fossil fuel production, then it doesn't make sense to support a company who makes money off of fossil fuel.**

So, the first step is to divest.

In my case, as an example, I personally do not invest in losers. I don't invest in business strategies that are profitable only at the expense of others, including gambling, payday types of loans, private prisons, or tobacco stocks. It doesn't mean these companies are bad, per se. Sure, I can argue that, but I have better things to do with my time. With a stroke of a pen, I write them out of my personal investment policy. This may provide lower returns than if I invested in them. Or it may not, it really all depends on the sectors or companies I exclude and the market forces on any given year. But when I take this step, I am not taking it for returns. I am excluding companies because I want money to be out in the world, if not doing good, at least not doing harm.

The benefit is that this is easy, transparent, and does no harm. It doesn't really require any special knowledge. The obstacle for some is that buying individual stocks requires a larger asset base. I tend to think an account needs at least $250K to delve into a basket of individual stocks. There are some mutual funds available that do this, but rarely do you find them in 401(k). And rarely does a 401(k) let you invest in individual stocks. Some 401(k) plans don't allow for it.

# THE SECOND STEP

Next stop on this roadmap to being more intentional about what your money is doing on your behalf? Determine what part of your portfolio will be in publicly traded companies that are addressing their ESG risks. This step is probably the most complex because it is not as black and white as step one. I should probably start by defining ESG investing.

Since the beginning of time, investors have looked at companies six ways to Sunday in an attempt to find an information edge and pick a winner. This type of due diligence has never been refuted as a viable avenue to investing. Now, we have more data about a company than ever before, including energy usage, employment data, and aspects of the supply chain. We have information on how companies are addressing the climate change, their social standing, their social capital, and the makeup of their boardroom. This data can be used to not only align an investors values to their investments, but, as importantly, it can be an indication of a company's long-term profitability.

Let's say I am looking at two semiconductor companies and they both had strong fundamentals (a fundamental analysis looks at a company's financial statements to assess liability, assets, profits, loss, cash flow, and revenue). I would rather invest in a semiconductor company that has developed a chip that uses 30 percent less water for cooling, even if it is trading lower on a given day, because I know it will have an edge long term. And yes, it also aligns to what I value—preservation of our earth and its natural resources. So, it's a slam dunk.

But then I learn that the more efficient chip is used by armies around the world to launch cluster bombs and I am not in favor of that, even though it may be a good revenue stream. Do I stop investing? Perhaps it depends on the company's involvement with these armies. It's not cut and dry. There are trade-offs with every investment in public companies. Even with these trade-offs, we can leverage the abundance of data reporting to make more informed decisions on not only how we want our money to be in the world but how likely our company will be profitable in the long run.

Study after study has shown ESG investing will perform as good or better than traditional investing styles. This makes perfect sense because the way we value companies has dramatically changed over time. In the 1980s and before, a company's value was based on things you could see and more easily value: tangible property like factories, vehicles, and equipment. Now the table has completely turned and, according to the Global Association of Risk Professionals, 80 percent of a company's assets are intangible, including brand, reputation, human capital, and relationships, and so are at risk from poor management of their environmental and social interactions.

ESG's information and style of trading has increasingly become available, making it much easier to find an advisor who invests in this way. The business case is equally strong, as is the case to support your values and vision for the world. Investing with an ESG approach may result in lower returns than the broad market or it may not. It really depends on your timeline and how the inclusive and exclusive screens are applied to a strategy.[8] The disadvantage is that publicly traded companies are large and the decisions they make are often pragmatic. There is no pure-play. All companies have room for improvement.

# STEP THREE

The next step is to consider investments in a private business that compassionately measures and values the people, communities, and environment that their operations impact—also known as conscious companies. If you are investing in these companies, that does make a difference. And it goes without saying, if you own or run a company, you should start at "home." Though this is a small-scale example, this is exactly what my Grandpa Abood did, using his grocery store to create connections and bolster the community.

---

8    Utilizing an ESG investment strategy may result in investment returns that may be lower or higher than if decisions were based solely on investment considerations.

# If you are looking to transform your company, this is a great model. Invest at home first.

For qualified investors that meet certain net worth qualifications, step three offers you the ability to invest in small- and medium-sized private companies that seek to elevate humanity through business. These companies may be selling something as simple as widgets, but they have a higher purpose than profits—they're stakeholders. They know with the right leadership and culture that values all human lives and the environment, profits will follow. They invest in the education programming of their employees and communicate honestly and fairly with their supply chain. This may be hard to imagine because most of our experiences are with big, faceless companies.

Although not available for outside investment, Jabian Consulting is the perfect example of a private business that fits in the Conscious Wealth framework. Cofounded by my friend Nigel Zelcer, he provides an alternative to the large, exhaustive consulting model that sends its employees on the road Monday through Friday. Nigel saw a better way to provide business leadership and strategy consulting that elevated the consultant and client; he decided they would only take on local projects. They invest in their team members and hire consultants who want to become leaders in their local communities. The clients know they are not hiring an outsider and a deeper trust develops. Nigel has transformed his business, modeling a better methodology for the industry. There are many fledgling companies with similar visions, but not the capital or leadership to get there. Finding such private investments may be an appropriate part of your portfolio.

Pros: The advantage of such an investment is that it is a purer play than mega-cap companies. A company of a few hundred people can really meld and create a culture. This culture can ripple out to the community and all the stakeholders. Moreover, it is arguably easier to build a conscious company once a company is established, but not as rigid as a mega-cap company.

Cons: Such investments, although direct, are not liquid. That means such investments could lock up your money for seven to twelve years. It takes patient-capital to allow such a business to flourish. It is a long-term play. Please note, not all private equity invests in conscious business. In fact, the average private equity model is anything but patient with their capital. Much like step two, you must look beyond the labels and really determine if the investment is supporting the development of a conscious business.

# STEP FOUR

Now, the fourth step is to consider allocating to impact investments. A lot of people throw around the words "impact investments," but I am using it here with a very specific definition; I am talking about investments that intentionally create a positive impact with some financial return, both of which can be measured succinctly. Therefore, the investment in a semiconductor company cannot be considered "impact" because its business model is not to improve the environment.

Using less water is simply a byproduct of their process. Much like the impact of exclusion of gambling stocks cannot really be quantified. It must hit the following three criteria to be an impact investment:

- Intention
- Financial return
- Measurement of impact

An example of an environmental impact investment would be a private company that purchases farms, timber tracts, mines, and other properties either in distress or at risk of being exploited. They continue to restore, protect, and rehabilitate the land with expert interventions and remediation. They can then convert and sell the land for ranching, sustainable farming, or timber harvesting. However they proceed with land use, the impact is measurable in the acres, trees, particle pollutants in water, etcetera. At times, they are even able to have tax credits that add to their overall profit range of 6 to 10 percent. This investment hits all three marks: intention, measurable impact, and financial return.

However, an investment in a company that makes biodegradable diapers is not an impact investment just because they make diapers that happen to be better for the environment. Likewise, an investment in a nonprofit that gives away diapers has no financial return. An investment in a company that creates loans to sell biodegradable diaper-making machines to remote villages—where the villages make these diapers, sell them to other villages, repay the loan, and more importantly, therefore create a downward trend in traditional diaper purchases in those regions which indicates how many traditional diapers will *not* be sitting in landfills, all while providing employment and professional opportunities for locals—is an impact investment.

What are the benefits of working with conscious businesses? It is an exciting time to be part of innovative solutions that combine philanthropy and business. It's a pure-play, therefore you can actually measure your impact. There are always unintended consequences, no matter what you do, but there is much less ambiguity around the good your investment is actually doing.

The only disadvantages are that this is an emerging field with fewer investment options. Most often, these investments are not available to the average investor. By nature, impact investments are long-term investments and lack the liquidity of a publicly traded stock. Also, you may not be able to access your money for a three- to ten-year lock-up period.

By taking these four steps and fortifying your investment policy, you will be able to approximate the answer. I find this vital because I am continuously looking at ways to release components in my life that detract from my energy and purpose.

**I am able to live lighter and more joyfully when I have a better understanding of what my money is doing even if I am sleeping.**

Following the roadmap to becoming conscious about the impact of your investments has a few pre-requisites. Normally when investing, you consider how much you need your money to grow and what type of cash flow is required to meet your goals. This becomes increasingly important when embarking on this roadmap. When investing for impact, this becomes even more of a salient issue. With each step, there are liquidity considerations and performance trade-offs that absolutely need to be taken into consideration. Therefore, as you are adding new types of investments, you need to be sure you are always solving for Y—how much growth you need and when. Beyond that, you will need to look at the liquidity restrictions and expected performance of the underlying investments to ensure they allow you to reach your financial goals.

# YOUR STORY

What is your money doing on your behalf? Do you know what you want it to be doing? I admit, it is a lot of work to track the impact your money is having out in the world, much less with your family, but I also believe it is part of the responsibility of having financial assets. Without a doubt, it will be worth it. The conversations with your family alone will pay dividends in the form of engagement and increased understanding. This alignment of your investments can also have outsized impact on others while still leading the life you want to live. For me, once I knew I had enough and deepened my work toward my purpose, this family conversation seemed like a no-brainer.

Of course, the biggest prerequisite is that you know your intended impact and preferably have it written down. You can break down that one big question with some smaller questions and construct a Family Matters Document for you and your family. You will be able to refer to it daily and during meetings, before big decisions, or when times get rough.

The following document questions will likely reveal interesting, helpful answers:

- What are our individual values? What values do we hold as a family?
- What is our individual three-year vision? Where do we want to be in three years?
- How can we measure the unfolding of our vision?
- How do we enhance and enrich the lives of each other within the family?
- As a family, how do we enhance and enrich the lives of others within society at large?
- What investment, insurance or other types of strategies do we need to consider to fulfill our individual and shared purpose?
- What professionals do we need to engage to fulfill our individual and shared purpose?

# LEVEL FOUR

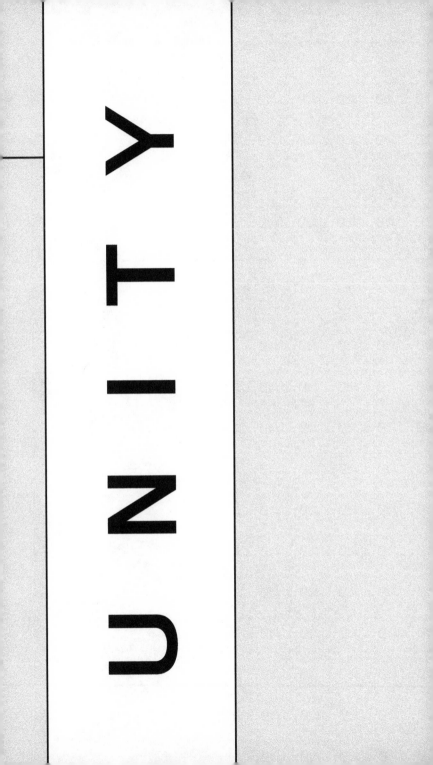

UNITY

# CHAPTER 9
# WHAT WILL I DO WITH MONEY THAT IS MORE THAN "ENOUGH"?

**I practice *Neelakantha* meditation.** Twice a day, I sit and cross my legs and internally place my focus on a mantra assigned to me. In other words, when thoughts and ideas come up that try to take my attention, I allow them to stay where they are while I gently return my focus to my mantra. While meditating this way, I take some pretty deep dives into consciousness—I don't know exactly where I go, but I am swimming around in this space that is kinda like an extension of the peaceful moment that occurs a few seconds right before you fall asleep. This is where my ideas come to me. This is where I see nothing and everything clearly. This type of blissful consciousness may happen for nineteen minutes of a twenty-minute meditation, or it may not occur at all during the entire session. It may elude me for weeks and then, bam, out of the blue, I sink into this deeper consciousness on a random Tuesday meditation session in my office at three p.m. Here is where I move outside of myself and find unity with all around me.

Working through the levels of Conscious Wealth's framework, you have hopefully come to internalize,

"I have enough." And, "I am enough!" With this awareness, you will likely want to share this abundance and purpose with others around you. Now it is time to consider unity, to question the concept of "I" as a separate entity. Meaning, the ownership of your money and your assets are called into question.

How did I get here? Me, a guy who spent his life focused on money?

# HOW I CAME TO A PLACE OF UNITY

Sometime back, when I played football and wrestled in high school, the L5 disk in my lower back became herniated. Years later, my doctor explained to me it was like a jelly donut with the jelly hanging out the side. There was no way to get the jelly back in. I just had to strengthen the muscles around the injury. I started yoga because of the back pain.

In fact, I had back pain from my work in the financial industry. Stress for me goes to my back. If I am not careful, I can be flat on my back for days due to a stressful episode. In my early years working in the big firm, I would lose two to three weeks of work annually to back pain. Incidentally, I also gained thirty pounds those first few years. A not so gentle reminder to me that it is particularly difficult to create wealth without destroying something else.

I showed up to yoga with my car's seat heaters on to numb the ache in my back. I was broken and in pain, thirty pounds overweight, though still oblivious to the underlying causes. One day, a friend who is a decade younger than me said he would never let that happen to him. I laughed and explained, "You don't let weight gain happen, you just wake up one day and realize it. Then you take years trying to reclaim your health."

I enjoyed the yoga and became quite committed to using it to heal my body. The instructor encouraged me to go to a meditation workshop. After a full day of teaching, I was enthralled by the language being used and the ideas. I promptly went to the teacher's website and signed up for his next session, three months later in San Francisco. I was going to one of the renowned spiritual centers in the world to learn from one of the greatest teachers how to meditate.

It was a magical weekend for me. I will always remember the day I was assigned a mantra and learned to meditate. It not only changed my life, but also, it was incidentally on Pi day—3:14:15. I was staying in the Tenderloin, then the seedier part of the city, and meeting at a commune in Haight-Ashbury with some very evolved human beings, just blocks from some of the richest individuals on planet earth. During that time, however, the client I mentioned in chapter 3, the one who spent like a drunken sailor and was generous with his kindness and love, was dying. The phone calls to him and his family kept me grounded. It was a "this and that" type of situation, where multiple contrasting realities were simultaneously present and equally true.

Through my meditation teacher, I was introduced to nondualistic thinking in spiritual relevance. At its highest level, it refers to a state of consciousness where you transcend your body and are united with one undivided spirit that is present in everything "living" and "dead." In practical terms, duality means there is a body and a spirit. It means that there are six billion separate beings on the planet. And that there is life and death—all of these things see the world as divided and separate.

Nonduality sees the world as one. It sees your body and spirit intricately combined, and at the same time it sees a connection with you and the spirit of all other six billion people on earth. Nonduality sees continuity of your spirit after death.

> **Nondualistic thinking is the underpinning of achieving a Conscious Wealth mindset. If "I" is really "we," then "my" money and assets are really "our" money and assets.**

There are many interesting facets to be unpacked around this type of unity and Conscious Wealth. Please, read on.

## YOU CAN'T TAKE IT WITH YOU

You've heard it before: you can't take anything with you when you die. Therefore, you are simply a custodian of the assets that under current earthly law are titled in your name, be it land, money, or businesses. Although earthly law or regulations may not always state it, you are a custodian of the planet and all its people. Your task is bigger than yourself, your purpose, and your family's purpose.

If this is your mindset, then the implications on *how* you invest, gift, and commit to philanthropy are far reaching.

"What will I do with the money that is more than what I have defined as enough for me?" is a real question in both life and death. For those of you with an excess of financial assets, there is an amount of money that you won't ever be able to spend. It's just too much. Even if everything goes wrong and you have to turn to plan Z with all the twists in turns of life, you won't run out of money.

I have seen others with far less money yet with the same issue of not being able to spend all their money in their lifetime. There is a limit to the joy and fulfillment you will get from spending money. Once you cross that limit, your choices are limited.

I work with clients who have lived a life of net spending $10K a month for years. After many decades of hard work and saving, they retire with enough money to spend multiples of that. But here's the kicker. They just don't. They continue to spend $10K a month. Perhaps they are not wired that way. Perhaps they don't find joy from it.

**Each family is different, but the fact remains, once you have more than enough, the question is about what to do with the rest?**

This is a real question. If you decide not to answer now and continue along your traditional route of investing while you think about it for a little longer, the issue will only compound with growth. Of course, there is a chance you will die before you've made a decision. When you do indeed leave this earth, the decision will have to be made. Hopefully, you have at least designed an estate plan to answer the question after your passing.

It's best to tackle these issues when alive, to not leave the hard decisions to those left behind. If you are approximating this state of "more than enough," then you are already living in a state of abundance more often than not—all of your financials are in order, you are grounded by a sense of a life of purpose, and you have assets allocated toward both growth and preservation.

Beyond these assets, practically speaking, you have three options for the direction of your money if you decide not to invest for strict financial return. They exist in both life and death. You can give your assets to people you know or people you don't know, usually via charities. Or, you can put it under your mattress and let it decay. Or invest it for growth and compound the issue at hand.

If we take ourselves out of the equation and look at it from the most logical sense, the best option is to give it away. You know, to set up our family and friends with enough to achieve their own sense of abundance and purpose and then put the rest out there in the world. Heck, Jesus did it. So did Buddha, St. Francis, St. Paul, and many others. I mean, what else would you do with all that money, just let it sit there?

I will freely admit this is not my natural tendency.

The thought of giving away so much makes me uncomfortably vulnerable. I may feel safe and secure now, but the excess of cash or assets can feel like a security blanket. Something to keep me safe. It is easier to tell myself I will invest it and let it grow so others can have more later. I know I can't take myself out of it completely. I am not a fully enlightened being and have fears and concerns. Nevertheless, I will not try to explain it away.

Although I am not fully ready to give it all away, I have accepted that it is what I consider the aspirational thing to do. However, I will not feel guilty or justify my actions for perhaps holding onto more than I may "need." Neither should you.

# BUT . . . CAN WE REALLY GIVE ANYTHING AWAY?

Yes, it's a weird, complicated question: can we really *give* anything away?

Pierre Teilhard de Chardin wrote, "We are spiritual beings having a human experience," and not the other way around. So, if we are just passing through and we indeed go on to another form of life or even no life at all, then our money, property, all our assets, well, it is out of our control. As was mentioned in the last section, it no longer belongs to us in death. We are just taking care of it for the short time we are on this planet. Here's why this is a scary thought . . . if it is not yours in death, how can it be yours in life?

Then you have to answer the question, whose is it really? Which also leads to the question, if you are being asked to take care of money, then is letting it pile up and then doing nothing shirking your responsibility?

Over coffee, I ask friends if we ever really own anything, and sometimes I get indignant retorts, like "So what? Are you just going to give it away? Then give it to me!" and my response is, "No, you are not getting it. If it is not mine, how can I consider it mine to *give* it away?"

It's a real bind. A bind I think a lot about and one I am still finding my way through.

Let's say you are the type of person who likes to give panhandlers money on the street and you toss some spare coins in the hat of the guy on the corner. To begin with, if you did this, oftentimes it is to make yourself feel better, more than this person. You may congratulate yourself and tell yourself that you are generous. Or you may feel guilty about how bad this person's life is. It may help this individual buy a warm cup of coffee and make his day a bit more pleasant. That same money may allow him to visit a professional organization that is trained and equipped to help him improve his life. None of this is wrong or makes you a bad person—that is far from the point. Yet if any of this holds true, you are actually just *giving* more to yourself than them.

On the other hand, let's say that you see countless people living on doorsteps in your neighborhood, and you are deeply saddened. You are moved to make a change, and you have the resources to do so. You use the money in your care to build a shelter that provides opportunities for people not living in homes. You win the support of the neighborhood, and your shelter is filled with volunteers and mentors. The community empowers the people without homes toward full employment, bank accounts, clean clothes, and their own homes. It is clear that you really did help that other human being, and she is no longer hanging outside your door. Indeed, homelessness in this part of town would have decreased because your shelter partially solved the local issue. Simultaneously, your property value in the neighborhood goes up.

Or perhaps you just created new customers to buy your company's product and have increased the commerce in your city. Not only did you get new customers, but now you have new access to a labor force who didn't exist and is increasingly hard to attain. The labor force is grateful and empowered and thus more productive.

Again, who is really giving here? Who is really receiving? *Can I ever really be successful if others around me are not?*

There just must be a better word than "giving" out there. A vocabulary limitation aside, here is what I have seen in my experience as an advisor: there is a mindset that you can adopt that earning more money will no longer make you wealthier—in fact, you could double your money and not be wealthier.

**When you release yourself of the need to make more money, you open yourself up to joy. You are no longer focused on making more money because you realize it no longer provides more joy.**

You are able to experience how true wealth comes as you empower others. You realize your greatest impact will always be when you seek the highest expression of who you are through both self-awareness and connection with others.

Conscious Wealth is a path, not a destination. You may be there on a Tuesday and have some fears triggered that take you off course on Wednesday. Yet, the more you remain in the space of security and comfort, the more likely you are able to get yourself back on track. Conscious Wealth is attained by being aware of your thoughts around money and consciously answering the tough questions. It is coming back to these questions time and again and answering them. It also is supported by action.

Whether giving to family or charities, it is important to keep the big picture in mind. If the purpose of the money you spend is to bring out your most authentic self, then the money you give to others should bring out the most authentic self in others. This is tricky because giving carte blanche can bring out the most inauthentic self of others. Imagine a twenty-year-old who's trust begins to kick out half a million dollars a year; it's easy to see how someone in that situation may not know to consider the implications of being rich versus being wealthy. Likewise, giving too many restrictions and hoops to jump through while trying to create an authentic attempt to make your giving more effective can create negative limitations and resentment.

So, how do you navigate this balance of giving freely enough to create authenticity but with enough guard rails to maximize the growth of the receiver?

# LOOK FOR GOAL ALIGNMENT

It makes little sense and provides little motivation to give to organizations and or people that do not hold the same core values as you. This doesn't mean you have to give only to like-minded people; they may think completely different than you and want to make changes that you never dreamt of. However, your efforts will be most effective if you focus on finding people who are like-hearted. People who see goodness in the world and want to bring it out more, whether it be through the arts, science, or education.

It does little good giving to organizations or people who are completely out for themselves or do not see the value in helping others. Finding organizations and family members with the mindset of helping others is not easy but vital.

# SEEK COLLABORATION

One of the biggest traps for well-intentioned donors is they want to reinvent the wheel or invest in a start-up nonprofit—it is widely understood that there is entirely too much overlap in nonprofits. It is fair to say many of this overlap is a result of competing egos or a desire to leave a legacy. What I suggest is that a Conscious Wealth philanthropist that has reached the level of Unity seeks to create mergers, acquisitions, and collaboration between nonprofits. Then seek to share resources and find solutions and credit.

# PLAN FOR LEARNING OPPORTUNITIES

Give small and slow before giving big and fast. This holds true for family members and charity. You can easily overwhelm people or nonprofits with more money than they are accustomed to spending. You can create mission drift. Small nonprofits may start to take on endeavors that don't fit neatly in their mission and family members may buy a Ferrari instead of paying for college.

**What may seem like a small amount of money for natives of wealth can seem like a fortune to immigrants to wealth. That is because in part they don't understand the power or limitations of wealth.**

Inheritors may see a $200K gift as a ticket to freedom, when others would be grateful for the inflow but not adjust their life in any way. The reason you start small is because people and nonprofits are going to stumble. They will need to learn their lessons. And it is best to learn big lessons with small consequences, then the other way around. It allows them to build up resiliency.

# DO IT WHILE YOU ARE ALIVE

The value of doing this in your lifetime is that you can be a source of coaching and guidance as the recipient(s) of your giving is acclimating to new territory. You have unique talents and knowledge that can guide your child as he starts up his first business. You can help mitigate the trend of families gaining and losing fortunes all within three generations. You can hire professionals to support your family. For example, you can hire executive coaches for your family member who wants to take over the business. You can be the advisor to a local nonprofit. You can do values and mission exercises with them and help them better understand and shape their values and your family values. You can sit on the board of the nonprofit that takes your donation to scale up its operations. On top of that, you can enjoy seeing your money allow others to live a more authentic and fulfilling life.

You can't do any of that when you are dead.

# HAVE A TAX PLAN

It's always good to have a tax plan. There are opportunities to maximize your gifts and minimize your taxes and they should absolutely be considered.

However, the sole purpose of estate planning is not to give as much money as humanly possible to your children and as little to the government. The purpose of family riches is not just to maintain it, but to give where it has the most positive impact. After all, deciding how much you are going to give your children should not be driven by taxes; you can jump through a million hoops and create trust after trust after trust, but what these legal documents and entities do is further entrench the "otherness." Money is creating walls instead of breaking them down.

A quick word on taxes—no matter how much you save on taxes, you are still net-net giving. No matter how big the tax break, you are still out of pocket when giving. So, instead, look at it this way: if you are going to give, why not take advantage of the tax laws, within reason.

Complaining about paying taxes is like complaining about your heartburn from the Dom you drank at the Ritz Carlton last night. Nobody wants to hear it. Smart tax planning makes sense, but in my humble opinion, it is not the end of the world to pay taxes. It means you made money. That is a good thing. If it bothers you that government is so inefficient, consider charitable donations going toward finding ways to strengthen our government and public systems. We live in a country that is touted as a democracy and is ridiculed for its ineffectiveness, but we can't have it both ways. Authentic steps to strengthen our public system are badly needed in collaboration with the private sector—not just to find a work-around—even if it undermines the very system that allowed you to build your wealth. It is too early to give up on democracy.

# PLAN FOR YOUR DEATH AS IF IT WERE TOMORROW

The best estate plans are the ones that are communicated to family members before your death. An estate plan will deal with the assets you did not spend in your lifetime. It can create guidelines for organizations and family members.

Hopefully, if you made it to the Unity level, your fear of dying has subsided enough to soberly make an estate plan. The nightmare situation is the one we see on television, where the family members sit in row in a mahogany-lined study of sorts, as an attorney reads the will of the deceased. It's almost comical how this scene is repeated over and over again in the movies. Ideally, you have built out your estate plan and have had a chance to discuss its structure with your family so that this scenario is not necessary.

**There should be no surprised gasps from family members if there does have to be a reading of the will.**

"What if my children find out how much money I have and get soft?" is more or less the fear many people have regarding sharing the details of their will. I ask them, "What if your children are already soft and unprepared for the future and only getting softer? Or worse, what if your kid ends up resenting you from the grave?"

# GIVING IS AN INVESTMENT

Keep in mind that a gift of money is still an investment. It is an investment for social return, not financial return. No matter whom you give to, it is fair to expect the recipient to do good for society and spread your shared core values. And like all investments, it is possible that you can have a concentrated position. "Concentrated position" is the technical term for saying "You've got all your eggs in one basket." You can give too much to one entity. This question on how much for one philanthropy and one child should be explored very seriously.

Philanthropy has traditionally been seen as strictly an investment for social return, but the landscape is changing. Nonprofits have always been a tax designation that allows companies that serve the common good to not pay taxes. The rationale behind that is they are performing services not profitable for the business world to take on. Yet, all along, they were expected to be run like businesses with one key difference—much of their revenue came from donations. While this is still the case and a much-needed tax designation, social entrepreneurs and established nonprofits are finding ways to integrate revenue models into their businesses. Moreover, some for-profit companies are being created with philanthropic-like ideals but without a donor base. Instead, they raise capital from investors and pay back with revenue models.

All of this is the exciting and burgeoning field of impact investments. Keep an eye out for it. If all of this giving sounds like business, that is because it is. Philanthropy, impact investing, or whatever comes next must be tracked. You should consider the sector, size, and style of your investments. You should consider trend lines, impact, entry strategies, exit strategies. You should have a relationship with the leadership teams you are giving to. You, and your family if giving as a unit, should have a Philanthropic Mission statement, even if you are not using a foundation to organize your giving. Much of this organizational structure can be found on my website in a tool my team created called the Impact Map. Honestly, it's a very helpful resource; you should check it out: brandonhatton.com/impact-map/.

So, what will you do with all the money you are unable to spend?

They say the typical rich family goes from "short sleeves to short sleeves" in three generations. The first generation creates a strong financial foundation, the second expands the foundation to a sizeable asset base, and the third generation spends it all.

What is powerful about guiding families to build and maintain Conscious Wealth, and why I see it as my task as an advisor, is twofold. The first is that it ain't pretty when families go from short sleeves to short sleeves. That is, the transition often involves addiction, abuse, suicide . . . and that is just the impact in the family. Outside, people lose jobs and their livelihood. Fortunes are wasted, and people are hurt.

On the other hand, when a family is able to preserve their wealth for many generations and use it to fulfill their individual purposes and the family purpose while helping society as a whole, well, the impact is undeniably positive. Businesses are built that serve people, charities deepen their support to societies' most vulnerable, and family members lead a life of fulfillment and leadership.

# GRATITUDE

How it all fits together—abundance, purpose, impact, unity—seems so magical to me.

Through my practice, I create impact by empowering others to deepen their impact. I do it in a way that respects them as individuals and simultaneously respects my truest self by allowing me to live my most authentic life as I serve others by integrating money, purpose, business, family, society, everything. The greatest gift of all is that I was able to do this from where I was at. I transformed my life by coming to peace with my Money Memories and allowing for abundance. I transformed my career by making bold choices, going back to the fundamentals, and choosing goodness. I continue to allow my journey with money to heal myself, my relations, and my work.

I was heading down a pretty destructive path a decade ago when I was sitting in the car alone, disconnected from my work, my friends, my family, and myself. I lacked unity because I was engrained in a commercial system that clearly stated every man for himself. I lacked purpose. I lacked Conscious Wealth.

### Now, I have enough. I live abundantly and with purpose.

I am headed to the correct shore with an unobstructed view. And I catch glimpses of the interconnectivity between all us. There is still so much more to explore within the four levels of Conscious Wealth and I am just beginning. Humility is required. If you believe you have completed the levels and reached the highest state of Conscious Wealth, indeed you have not. It is the work of a lifetime.

Increasingly, I see my efforts less in terms of giving. I don't "give" anymore. I am an investor after all. I invest my talents within my company to empower all stakeholders: my clients, my teammates, and our network of professional advisors. As an investment manager, I have a portfolio that only invests in companies that actively address their social and environmental risks when operating a profitable business. I invest in companies trying to solve the world's most deeply rooted problems. I invest my time in training my teammates because I want them to grow as professionals. I invest in charity's missions (although IRS codes state I am actually donating money). I invest in family members so they can have an impact in the world with less financial constraint. I invest, I invest, I invest . . .

I do this with love. And I do all this empowering with the fundamental understanding that there is a potential return on my investment for me because when I empower others, I empower myself. And not in the sense that what goes around, comes around. There's no quid pro quo—I am others, and others are me.

That's Conscious Wealth.

So, what am I going to do with all my money and assets?

First of all, I'd like to bounce my last check and swallow my last quarter, but as I said before, I never know when that ice cream truck full of Reese's Peanut Butter Klondike bars is barreling down the road with my name on it. Therefore, I will invest in myself and others, with a clear understanding of the risks yet without fear of loss. And I will invest in people and organizations with an expected return, perhaps social, perhaps monetary. And I will continue to invest until there is no separation between me and you.

# YOUR STORY

Conscious Wealth is in your grasp. Take a moment to reflect on the following questions and use your answers to turn your financial plan and desire to heal around money into action:

- What am I going to do with all my assets I am unable to spend?
- How do I support the authentic expression of others?
- How does my estate plan support the most authentic expression of others?
- Who knows about my estate plan? How can I communicate to others the details of my estate plan so that they can lead a more authentic life?
- How do I do Philanthropy? Do I have a strategy? Who do I give to? How do I track my impact?
- What grade would you receive as the custodian of your financial assets?
- Are my heirs ready to receive any inheritance? What can I do to empower them to be more prepared?

# CHAPTER 10

# HOW DO YOU HEAL YOUR RELATIONSHIP WITH MONEY THROUGH FAMILY VALUES?

**To illustrate the journey to adopting the Conscious Wealth mindset, I'd like to introduce you to the Smith family.** Now, the Smith family is not an actual family, but rather a combination of families I know and money stories I've heard that I'd like to use to illustrate my point. So, while this case study is hypothetical, it is realistic.

Why do I do this? Let me tell you, there was no shortage of criticism when I personally decided to restructure my life from the world of greed to a role of serving others. Resistance from change will always exist. The question I ask myself is this: why are they resisting change?

## MEET THE SMITH FAMILY

The Smith family had a construction company three generations deep. They were well known and trusted in the industry. For decades, they had a narrow but effective way to make a difference—through the power of business. They treated their employees with dignity and generously compensated them to build quality homes for other people to safely live in. Smith construction was founded by Mary Smith's father. Mary, her husband Mike, and their daughter Stella ran the family business. Their son, Jackson, had little interest in the business world, and in money in general. He gravitated toward art.

# HOW MUCH IS ENOUGH?

The Smith family approached me and had no idea how much their business was worth. This was troubling, as almost all of their financial net worth was tied up in the business.

"If we sold Smith Construction, would we have enough to retire?" Mike Smith asked me.

After spending years in the trenches building up a business, business owners often have two questions: How much can I sell this for? Is that enough?

We started at the beginning. We examined the Smith family's goals, financial net worth statement, cash flow statements, retirement projections, business evaluations, tax strategies, basic estate planning, and insurance strategies. Yes, it was a lot of data. We also worked with a business valuation consultant to get a better handle on the value of their business.

Over the following eighteen months, we fine-tuned their financial plan by uncovering the unknowns. The most important factor and unknown was how much they actually spent each year. Furthermore, how much they wanted to spend in the future after considering their family goals. Perhaps the biggest unknown? How much they would be able to cash out by selling their company.

The business evaluation experts pointed out some easy and some more challenging modifications to the business that would push the price of the company up dramatically. The family listened to the feedback and endeavored to make the bulk of those changes, working steadfastly toward an exit from their life's work.

Meanwhile, we discovered rather quickly that the Smith family was headed in a direction that would yield more than they could or even want to spend in one lifetime.

It was a fantastic discovery. Yet, in so many ways, it was evident they'd already sensed this reality. They had adopted a secure and abundant mindset and the conscious business they were running was evidence of that. Furthermore, they generously gave money to charities in their community and supported many causes they cared about. That family celebrated their success and the success of others. They lived a great lifestyle but did not feel compelled to prove their success or wealth to others or themselves.

## WHAT TO DO

"If I'm in a position to do anything in the world, what do I really want to do?" they asked themselves.

Through the sale of their business, the Smith family had more money than they could spend in one lifetime. It is a problem we all wish we could have, but it does not come without some serious questions.

Perhaps the biggest question was: how much, if anything, would they gift their children? The family was split on this issue. Mary believed the private education, annual gifting, and the help on a down payment for a house was more than enough, while Mike wanted to structure it so Stella and Jackson did not have to toil as much as Mike and Mary had the past.

It is a common disagreement and a delicate balance. How much was enough to provide opportunities but also without stripping their children of the pleasure of achievement?

**Another important but commonly divisive question was in regards to how they would live their lives with the wealth now available to them.**

It is common for a family to sell a company, say worth $50MM, and one spouse wants to start making friends with other people with that level of wealth, or perhaps with the billionaire crowd (believe it or not, these are actually two different crowds). Meanwhile, the other spouse wants to hold onto the friends they've always had. Many times, one or both spouses want to pretend the money is not there, or that everything is still the same. This can be quite destructive for their relationships with each other and with friends, if for no other reason than it is not true. Luckily for Mike and Mary, they were going into this with eyes open and unified.

Additionally, the sale of the Smith business was going to cause a big shake-up in the family. For instance, both Mary and Mike would never have to work again, although Mike did want to start a boutique eco-construction business as a passion project. Their daughter Stella would need to find a new job, as the sale of the business would render her financially stable for now, yet unemployed. As for Jackson, well, he wouldn't be directly impacted at all. He wasn't involved with the business, the money, or even the family that much.

Knowing these challenges were coming, I gave them a card game I'd designed called Family Matters. It consists of twenty-six questions about money and life. Questions include: What are your family's top three values? How do you know? If you could spend a day doing anything you wanted, what would you do? And money is . . . (fill in the blank).

Over a few Sunday dinners, they pored over the cards and had some amazing conversations. When it was time for our next meeting, they had quite a bit of clarity around their future.

They stated their values as integrity, hard work, service, and humility.

Then they started to dream aloud. Mary about retiring, watching the grandkids, and writing children's books. Mike about opening the boutique construction company that builds cabins fully integrated into the environment. Stella wanted to stay in the industry and continue working. While Jackson was enjoying the conversations and opportunities to see a different side of his parents, he at first thought of this discussion about money very separate from the purpose of his art and his life.

As the family began to think about how they wanted

to create an impact in the world beyond them, Jackson became intrigued. The Smith family saw business as an avenue to make a difference in the world. Now, with the sale of their business, there was a yearning to continue to find ways to make a bigger impact. They had always envisioned a world with economic opportunity, affordable and safe housing. Through discussion, all members of the family agreed that supporting opportunities for women and cultivating freedom of expression and art were also important to them.

**Quite informally, they did it. They defined what they stood for, what they wanted out of life and how they wanted to make the world better.**

We solidified it with a Family Matters Document and got to work. We began by creating a business succession, financial, investment, insurance, and philanthropic plan around the guidance they provided. We guided them through the sale of the business and planned for what I call a "victory lap." They traveled, visited family and friends, and did not make any major financial decisions for one full year.

A year later, they returned inspired and ready to review, refine, and implement their plans. Mike opened his boutique shop and had a goal to build three houses a year. Mary took to the lifestyle of grandparenting with joy. This was particularly helpful, because they negotiated a deal that Stella would stay on with the new company for two years. This would provide her an opportunity to build up some capital to either start her own company or pursue another route.

Together, Mary and Mike decided to open both an LLC that could fund for-profit enterprises and a donor-advised fund for the funding of nonprofits. Perhaps the most rewarding aspect of all was Jackson's personal growth throughout this journey. The exercises around values and vision brought him closer to his family and inspired him to learn more about the family finances. Jackson worked with the lead advisor to learn more about the family business and where he could have a personal impact. Mary and Mike hired a personal coach for Jackson to solidify his vision. He was engaged in the family philanthropy, and eventually led the family meetings around giving. With a demonstrated commitment, they paid him a salary for this work. This was his first steady income and provided him with the necessary lessons around money. It allowed him to earn money but not at the expense of his deepest desires and passion around making art. This was good, because his parents decided not to leave him or his sister enough money to be independently wealthy, just enough to get a great start.

**Over the years, the family found increasingly more joy and fulfillment from investing in their vision for the world—whether that was in public companies, conscious businesses, impact investing, or nonprofits.**

When they were young, Mike and Mary used to joke, like me, they wanted to bounce their last check and swallow their final quarter. Now, they kind of meant it. They were hell-bent on spending and giving away all their money.

The family's growth was humbling.

They have a more harmonious, aligned, purposeful family that is making a difference in ways they never imagined. Each family is imbued with abundance and purpose. The donor-advised fund they established is serving as a vehicle to deepen their connection to others and empower the purpose of others. They meet at least once a year to discuss their family matters and take an annual vacation together. They still have struggles, challenges and tension as all families do, but they are flourishing and communicating.[9]

There is a sample Family Matters Document at the end of this chapter, using the hypothetical Smith family to role model what your answers could look like. My clients have found this to be hugely helpful, as I hope you will.

---

9   Donors are urged to consult their attorneys, accountants or tax advisors with respect to questions relating to the deductibility of various types of contributions to a donor-advised fund for federal and state tax purposes.

# YOUR STORY

This is a simplified version of my Family Matters Document, but it gets to the heart of the matter. I encourage you to create a sample document for yourself and sit down with your family as soon as possible. Happy connecting!

• • • •

## THE SMITH FAMILY

## Family Matters Document

### Values
- Integrity
- Justice
- Meaningful Work
- Perseverance

### Family Mission Statement
We support ourselves and one another to build a more loving and equitable world.

### Personal Vision Statements
**Mary:** I am a loving grandmother, retiring business woman, and future community activist.
**Goal:** To allow my next chapter to unfold.

**Mike:** I support my family and my community through love and service.
**Goal:** To open a boutique eco-construction and have "work-fun"

**Stella:** I am a mom, wife, and business woman. I love adventure and growth.
**Goal:** To build my own construction company through the knowledge and resources I have been granted.

**Jackson:** I am a musician and artist.
**Goal:** To help these losers give away their money. Just kidding. To perform on every continent and have my art experienced by millions. To learn more about philanthropy.

### Family Goals

- Successfully exit the company in a tax efficient manner that supports our children, employees, and our charitable endeavors.
- Secure a retirement lifestyle that includes travel, healthcare expenses, and our discretionary and nondiscretionary needs—as detailed in our plan.
- Invest for financial and social return—aligned with our values and our vision for the world.
- Develop a Giving Strategy with goals, metrics, and governance. We want to experience the joy of empowering others during our lifetime.
- Create and refine an estate plan that provides our children with opportunities that previous generations did not have and also encourages them to achieve more.

# CONCLUSION

My hope is that through appraising your Money Memories and discovering the important aspects of each level of Conscious Wealth, you are able to change your story and—like the Smith family—live with abundance, purpose, impact, and unity. To live your life fully.

My meditation teacher explained to me the analogy of the wave and ocean. The idea is that each of us are waves in this grand sea of life. No wave is expected to be like other waves. And the purpose of meditation for us custodians living in the world is not to quell the wave, but to dip down into the sea and be connected to the great source that every other wave is connected to. Then we must come back up to the surface, after meditation, and splash around. The idea is that the waves are not separate from one another, nor is the wave separate from the ocean. It is all one. It is non-dual, in spiritual terms.

The analogy of the wave and ocean brings me comfort. The tense energy I hold in my chest is released into a deep exhale when I think of it. Just like the wave that quells and dips into the ocean, I have explored so many corners of my life while exploring my story of money in order to write this book. I have also asked you to do the same. Now, it is written. I do not have to relive those experiences every day nor continue to hash up old Money Memories. The discoveries I've made while writing have given me the nourishment, solid ground, peace, and the ability to live with less encumberments of the past. With this strength, I am also liberated to celebrate both my individuality *and* my oneness with humanity. I can work, convene, invest, love, play, heal—all of this through my actions or just through me being me.

In other words, I am free to rise from the depths of the ocean and splash around.

I wish you the same. Splash!

*Brandon*

# ACKNOWLEDGMENTS

I'd like to give thanks to my clients, who have been my unsuspecting teachers over the years. I am so fortunate to work with such a talented, loving, diverse, and successful group of human beings. Thank you for the trust you have given to me, as well as the opportunity to grow through service.

I would also like to acknowledge the many financial industry professionals I have met throughout my career who are role models, going to work each day with humility and the desire to serve their clients.

I could not have written this book if it were not for all the people along the way who supported me. Thank you to my friends who read early copies and provided feedback. Wayne South Smith and Mary Anna Rodabaugh for helping me write my story. And for editing, Holly at Lorincz Literary Services. Vince Caine for his continuous support of me and of my nontraditional wealth management practice. I would also like to thank the team at Conscious Capitalism Press for getting my book out into the world.

At all times, I believe in knowing what I own, why I own it, and how much it could cost me. The more confident I am in the purpose and impact of my investments, the more at peace I am, pursuing a life of purpose.

—BRANDON HATTON, CAP, CRCP, Family Wealth Advisor

# ABOUT THE AUTHOR

A consistent, process-driven individual, Brandon enjoys the fulfillment that working with people brings, reveling in the quixotic, creative, methodical nature of portfolio creation and wealth maintenance based on Conscious Wealth practices.

Brandon specializes in family dynamics around multi-generational wealth and is well-versed in advising clients on how to use their financial assets to help make a positive societal impact, whether through investments or philanthropy. This can include facilitating an exit from a company, a transfer of wealth, or preparedness for the next generation. He endeavors to help his clients live an abundant life with intention. For him, an intentional way of life includes knowing personal goals as well as acknowledging what it will take to reach them, and then doing the work.

Brandon has traveled the world many times over, opened a school in Egypt with a team of four others and taught history in Lebanon and Brazil.

In his free time, Brandon enjoys sailing, riding his bike, and practicing his culinary arts on his own recipes in his own kitchen or over an open fire. Originally from Cleveland, Ohio, he makes his home in Atlanta, cultivating healing through Conscious Wealth in himself and in others.

BRANDON
HATTON

# ELEVATE HUMANITY THROUGH BUSINESS.

Conscious Capitalism, Inc., supports a global community of business leaders dedicated to elevating humanity through business via their demonstration of purpose beyond profit, the cultivation of conscious leadership and culture throughout their entire ecosystem, and their focus on long-termism by prioritizing stakeholder orientation instead of shareholder primacy. We provide mid-market executives with innovative learning exchanges, transformational storytelling training, and inspiring conference experiences all designed to level-up their business operations and collectively demonstrate capitalism as a powerful force for good when practiced consciously.

We invite you, either as an individual or as a business, to join us and contribute your voice. Learn more about the global movement at www.consciouscapitalism.org.

CPSIA information can be obtained
at www.ICGtesting.com
Printed in the USA
FSHW011814151021